HOT DISH HEAVEN

HOT DISH
Heaven

Classic Casseroles
from Midwest Kitchens

Ann L. Burckhardt

INTRODUCTION BY KARAL ANN MARLING

MINNESOTA HISTORICAL SOCIETY PRESS

Karal Ann Marling's essay is excerpted from a longer work originally commissioned by Northern Clay Center, Minneapolis, Minnesota, for the catalog/cookbook published in conjunction with the 1995 juried exhibition, Minnesota Hot Dish. The exhibition and cookbook were supported in part by a generous grant from Land O'Lakes, Inc.

www.mhspress.org

The Minnesota Historical Society Press is a member of the Association of American University Presses.

Manufactured in the United States of America

10 9 8 7 6 5 4 3

∞ The paper used in this publication meets the minimum requirements of the American National Standard for Information Sciences—Permanence for Printed Library Materials, ANSI Z39.48–1984.

International Standard Book Numbers
ISBN 13: 978-0-87351-568-9 (paper)
ISBN 10: 0-87351-568-4 (paper)

Library of Congress Cataloging-in-Publication Data
Burckhardt, Ann
    Hot dish heaven : classic casseroles from midwest kitchens / Ann L. Burckhardt; Introduction by Karal Ann Marling.
        p. cm.
Includes index.
    ISBN-13: 978-0-87351-568-9 (pbk. : alk. paper)
    ISBN-10: 0-87351-568-4 (pbk. : alk. paper)
    1. Casserole cookery. 2. Cookery, American—Midwestern style. I. Title.
    TX693.B84 2006
    641.8'21—dc22   2006019084

 # Contents

Preface

ANN L. BURCKHARDT

Feeding people has been an important theme in my life. When not cooking for my family and friends, trying a new restaurant, or curled up with a good cookbook, I'm dishing out recipes and nutrition information. A year of researching and taste-testing casseroles went into the book you now hold in your hands.

Who did I write this book for? Anyone who loves a meal in a casserole dish, hot from the oven.

For seniors, there have been many hot dish family favorites, like the beef-noodle mixture a friend of mine recalls as "Ladies Aid Hot Dish," because his mother served it every month when she went to Ladies Aid at their church; or the casserole that his wife fondly remembers simply as "Vegetable Dish"—that was, ironically, mostly meat—that combined beef, home-canned tomatoes, and whatever other vegetable was handy in the house. Or my own traditional dessert *en casserole:* Mom's thrifty, but delectable, bread pudding.

For the baby boom generation, casseroles are laden with nostalgia. One look, one whiff, takes them back to the family kitchen of the 1960s and 1970s, where as young children and teenagers they waited, plates at the ready, a hot dish in the center of the table and the inevitable question from their homemaking mom: "Have you washed your hands?"

For today's busy parents, hot dishes are a time-saver. You mix the meat, its accompanying starch and vegetable, and the sauce of choice. It matters not whether you do your own preparation or use one of the new make-and-take services. Once you've popped the dish in the oven, you have an hour to unwind, help with homework, watch the news, and prepare a salad or dessert, if you like. After the oven works its magic, melding flavors and coaxing tenderness, the simple dish makes its own magic, satisfying our hunger for good food and family solidarity.

For savvy singles, sharing a pan of lasagna or a cassoulet after work or to celebrate the weekend is a great way to connect and catch up with friends. For the beginning cook, even a hot dish with just five or so ingredients comes across as cool and competent, not to mention an affordable choice

1

to save cash for the next yoga or salsa dancing class.

Casseroles work nicely for families where everyone cooks—or at least helps. Mom and Dad can share the chopping and stir-frying, kids can measure and mix. Hungry teenagers, so adept at reading directions on frozen pizza boxes, can certainly put the casserole a parent has assembled the night before into the oven after school. And the thanks and praise for "getting dinner started" just might lead a teen to make a filling batch of Tater Tot Hot Dish on his own. And every family should learn a favorite hot dish to share at church, neighborhood, or sports team potlucks.

What follows is a celebration of the hot dishes of the Midwest heartland: Iowa, North and South Dakota, Minnesota, and Wisconsin. I feature some of the best casseroles served up in midwestern homes of the fifties, sixties, and seventies. These over seventy recipes, updated and kitchen-tested, fill chapters on classics, potlucks,

comfort food, side dishes, breakfast, and desserts. A seventh chapter, "Round the World in a Casserole Dish," travels from Afghanistan to Mexico via Europe. Follow the directions closely and you'll find the recipes all but foolproof. Since most folks enjoy a good story, I have woven personal and culinary history into the recipe introductions.

This book is dedicated to the cooks who stayed true to their hot dish favorites, such as scalloped potatoes with ham, corn pudding, and rice custard, even when the rest of the country turned to more complicated recipes and flavors. While trendier cooks saved time first by heating TV dinners, zapping microwave meals, stir-frying bagged ingredients, and, finally, eating more than half their meals at restaurants or ordered take-out, these cooks stayed the casserole course.

So . . . welcome to Hot Dish Heaven. It's a pleasant place to be.

O Casserole!

KARAL ANN MARLING

O casserole! O hot dish! O covered-dish supper! Surprise, surprise. Lift the lid and savor the cloud of fragrant steam. Celery? Or cream of celery soup? Mushrooms. Yes, button mushrooms. A little wine. Speckles of red pimento for color, for eye appeal. Green pepper, too, like edible confetti. Festive flecks of red and green. And fat white noodles, poised on the edge of culinary oblivion. Ten minutes more, at 325 degrees, and they'd have been glop, anonymous essence of casserole, as thick and gluey as library paste. O casserole!

There ought to be a law: noodles and soup must always come to the table in a rounded dish. Because squarish casseroles evoke lasagna. Hearty, peasant food, the cookbook writers say. We know better. Lasagna pans adopt superior airs. Even when made with cans of things plucked straight from the supermarket shelf, the finished concoction approximates some distant memory of ethnic haute cuisine. The Medici, perhaps. There was a recipe once, propped up on a sturdy *tavola* in a *cucina* back in faraway *Italia*. Things are layered in the dish, precise, distinct and smug.

When they don't contain lasagna, rectilinear casseroles cry out for asparagus spears, somehow, and casserole holders of silverplate with little canted legs and handles in the shape of metal bunnies or zucchini. Candles and a linen tablecloth. Faux elegance: asparagus and brie and buttered crumbs of crusty bread that doesn't come in plastic. There's something snooty about casseroles with corners.

But the whole point of casseroles—rounded ones; lovely circles and ovals—is a commingling of ingredients: chance encounters between tuna and potato chips; peas rubbing elbows with macaroni; a passionate adagio performed by the bashful onion sliver, which all but melts into the dancing throng of rice grains, and the exotic water chestnut, standing proud and crunchy to the end. A great democratic dance of colors, textures, flavors, all mixed up together in the pot, whirling as one in the heat of the oven. Real American food. The melting pot. *E pluribus unum.* Forget the apple pie. It's God, mother, and hot dish, in that order. God made mothers and mothers make casseroles.

3

FOOD SNOBBERY reached America soon enough, despite the self-evident excellence of beans. The rise of consumerism in the 1800s, for instance, meant that metal vessels were readily available in the Victorian kitchen, even on the western frontier, on the banks of the Mississippi. Mark Twain's Huck Finn complains that the widow who adopts him cooks everything alone, in its own pan, for the sake of gentility. He prefers baked beans and casseroles. "In a barrel of odds and ends it is different," Huck opines. "Things get mixed up, and the juice kind of swaps around, and the things go better." Home, he seems to be saying, is a place where the juice rises as a mouth-watering steam when your mother takes the lid off the casserole. A place where folks and feelings swap around, like onions and beans in a shiny brown and white pot.

In a sense, the casserole is the opposite of Jell-O. First patented in 1845 by Peter Cooper, Jell-O was only the longest-lasting manifestation of a Victorian mania for elaborate molded foods that connoted high culture by the difficulty of their preparation. As a proof of her cooking skills (or her maid's), the housewife was expected to turn out dainties shaped like gems and crowns and the Father of His Country. Although pretty blancmanges and ices predated the nineteenth century, they came into vogue again with the technology for stamping seamless molds out of metal that made the contents easy to turn out intact. Cold salad courses with perfect fillets of fish and slices of carefully shaped and peeled carrot suspended in mayonnaise often contained as many disparate ingredients as any casserole but the appeal was to the eye as much as to the quivering nose or to the palate. Molded salads and desserts are beautiful. Fussy. Casseroles, by contrast, are careless, messy things: mixtures of God-knows-what, stirred up and then concealed within the depths of a pot.

In frontier outposts, where molded salads awaited the coming of the railroad and the relentless march of civilization, the decorative cuisine taught in Boston cooking schools was impossible to practice anyway. The typical household had a frying pan, and an iron pot with a trivet inside for use as an impromptu bake oven. And that was that. Iron pots didn't break on the trek westward. Iron pots and the absence of most starches save flour favored the consumption of stews, loose versions of casseroles, assembled from whatever came to hand, boiled, thickened slightly in the gravy. Or soups, wetter still. A bouillabaisse, a classic hunter's stew eaten in every culture that adjoins a lake, a forest, or a plain. No recipe required. No course of lessons at a cooking school. No book of "receipts" and household tips for making radishes into roses.

Early cookbooks presuppose the existence of an oral tradition, some atavistic aptitude for making simple suppers. The *Book of Cookery* young Martha Custis (the future Martha Washington) got when she married Daniel Custis in 1749 had no advice whatsoever to offer on the practicalities of stewing squirrels or baking beans. Instead, the volume was full of instructions for making complicated dainties like "candy of angelico" or "sirrup of violets." Based on tidbits supposedly served to seventeenth-century aristocrats,

Mistress Custis' cookbook amounted to a kind of self-improvement tract, calculated to bring grace and refinement to the Virginia wilderness. It showed how great ladies cooked, or ate, in faraway places.

Ladies' luncheon cuisine of this ilk survived intact into modern times. Myra Waldo, author of the important *Casserole Cookbook* (1963), cautions her readers to avoid the temptation to gussy up a simple one-dish menu with "feminine, gooey salads with gobs of mayonnaise or whipped cream, or sticky combinations of canned fruits and chopped nuts and maraschino cherries. . . ." In *Onions in the Stew,* humorist Betty MacDonald, whose books on food and family were runaway bestsellers in the 1940s and '50s, makes fun of the "lumpy salads" served by the neighbor women on special all-girl occasions, such as baby showers: tuna fish "and marshmallows and walnuts and pimento (just for the pretty color, our hostess explained later when she was going to give us the recipe) and chunks of pure white lettuce and boiled dressing." The only thing worse, MacDonald says, are their fancy suppers, built around a ring mold of mushroom soup, hard-boiled eggs, and canned shrimp— the kind that taste like Lysol—set off by another mold of lime green Jell-O.

The casserole thrives in eras when appearances count for less. In the 1930s, with food a scarce commodity, Americans prized dishes that were inexpensive, soft, comforting, bland, and dependably the same, whatever the economic climate. Franco-American spaghetti and Kraft macaroni and cheese: de facto casseroles that started their journey to the table in tins and boxes. World War II and ration-ing elicited the first major crop of printed recipes for casseroles, recommended on grounds of both patriotism and economy. Writing from France in 1942, M. F. K. Fisher endorses the home economists' recent push for one-dish meals "or, less genteelly, a casserole," as a means of using up hard-to-come-by leftovers. Dice leftover ham into a casserole of cheese and macaroni, she suggests, or add it to a mixture of cooked noodles and canned mushrooms, browned in fat.

Fisher was somewhat skittish about white sauce, with which her grandmother's generation had blanketed nearly every comestible in order to purify and control the unruly variety of nature. But white sauce (or tomato, for the adventurous) made an excellent casserole base. Ida Bailey Allen, the well-known composer of giveaway cookbooks for Coca-Cola, published her *Money-Saving Cook Book: Eating for Victory* during the war years as a guide to preparing family meals with no waste, utilizing foodstuffs grown in backyard gardens. Her solution? Escallops. Casseroles. Noodles with hamburger, tomato sauce, almost any combination of homegrown vegetables, and buttered crumbs from yesterday's toast on top. Fish and macaroni in white sauce, seasoned with ends of cheese. Tuna (easier to get than meat) and corn flakes and this and that.

Before the war, even cookbooks for the frugal had described such dishes as "the dreaded scallops." Nor were instructions for their preparation liable to make the reader salivate in anticipation of dining on various quantities of meat scraps and stock, cooked cabbage, stewed tomatoes, and bread cubes, baked indefinitely. But the thick pottery casseroles themselves were considered so "quaint" and artistic-looking that even the cheapest ingredients arrived at the table with a certain panache also attached to the chafing dishes, or clunky earthenware pots set on copper tripods, on which bachelors, bohemians, and career girls entertained in rented rooms. A spirit lamp heated the casserole and warmed the mixtures of melted cheese or cream sauce and precooked foods. Sometimes known as the frying pan that "got into society," the casserole dish on the metal stand conveys a spirit of "hearty welcome and good cheer," declared the magazine cooking expert who wrote the 1903 classic, *Salads, Sandwiches and Chafing Dish Dainties*.

But the casserole—the vessel and what goes in it—really came into its own after World War II, along with the cans of Campbell's cream-of-something soup which, as Betty Fussell remarks in her tribute to America's four great postwar chefs of TV and newspaper fame, are "expressive of our mobile homes and mobile foods." It was an age of mobility, the era that invented dips for fast, efficient eating at cocktail parties, where the guests circulated, and munched, and never sat down. The busy hostess loved the casserole because, at last, she could go to her own party. It was an age of speed and the casserole could be made in the time it took to open a can, turn on the oven, and sip a martini.

Everything was there, in one container that fit in the top rack of the dishwasher. And it could be frozen ahead of time, in the top compartment of the new turquoise Kelvinator. The casserole dish was the wedding present of choice in the 1950s, proudly displayed in the room dividers that demarcated the open-plan kitchen from the rest of the ranch house in suburbia. Ceramic casseroles. Copper ones (that needed polishing, alas). Pyrex. Enamel on steel, in brilliant turquoise.

To frazzled women who work, the casserole is a godsend. Nora Ephron likes cooking after a hard day at the office because "there is something comforting about the fact that if you melt butter and add flour and then hot stock, *it will get thick!* It's a sure thing . . . in a world where nothing is sure." And just as surely as flour and butter and broth will always make a sauce, so a sauce (or soup) with noodles and a can of tuna and a cup of peas will always make a tasty casserole. It's foolproof and easy and a reassuring link with the past. With mother's turquoise casserole dish, and father humming quietly with contentment as he scrapes the last crispy morsels onto his plate.

The casserole amounts to a national memory: the All-American Casserole. Tuna with potato chips is a part of folklore now, the distilled essence of childhood and warm kitchens and love. When recipes for tuna hot dish begin to turn up in cookbooks in the 1980s, it signifies a rupture of connections with families and trust and simple joys—sons and daughters who have moved away and turned to sushi and Cajun-style redfish composed against a backdrop of greens with unpronounceable names. Forget the tuna lurking under chips: cholesterol, don't you know. Sad reading, those recipes for what we used to know by heart.

What would Thanksgiving be without thawed green beans, cream soup, and milk baked for 30 minutes, topped with a can of french-fried onions, and given a final turn under the broiler? The Holiday Classic Casserole. The recipe on every can of onions, to be thankful for. But everybody knows just how to place the onions for maximum effect.

Is one ever closer to the Deity than when consuming Tater Tot Casserole, plucked from the spiral-bound pages of any church cookbook ever sold in the vestibule after the morning service? The First Baptist Church of Laramie, Wyoming, celebrated its 120th anniversary in 1990 with a typical book of "remembrances and recipes." They go together, those two ingredients, like hamburger, mushroom soup, and Tater Tots. Or chow mein noodles, if that's all you've got in the house on a cold Thursday afternoon, after Oprah, with the school bus due any minute. On a Friday night, all alone, after a killing week at work. On a Sunday noon, right after church, when your parents stop by to chat. O blessed casserole!

EVERYBODY MAKES 'EM. The not-so-famous and the almost-famous. In a recent article about a former White House press secretary who, at the age of 71, has acquired a houseful of surrogate teenage children, *People* magazine confides that Luci Baines Johnson, daughter of the late president, came to the rescue with many casseroles. Of course she did, bless her heart! Casseroles make houses into homes, and people into families, communities, and countries. O casserole! Faithful casserole!

Casserole Classics

EVERY FIELD HAS ITS CLASSICS. There are classic books; Mark Twain's *Tom Sawyer* comes to mind. And there are classic works of art, such as the *Mona Lisa.* Movies? Why *Gone with the Wind,* of course. The recipes that I consider classic casseroles are featured in this chapter. These recipes are the backbone of the bake-and-serve tradition. They are the dishes we turn to again and again because everyone loves them. And because we've made them so often, we can put the ingredients together quickly and easily. Many of these casserole classics are basic combinations, which can be—and have been—revamped in all sorts of ways. Take macaroni and cheese, for example. This filling, golden mixture can be found at the supermarket, both packaged and frozen; every cafeteria and hometown eatery serves it. Yet cooks still prepare their family's favorite version. And sometimes they make some inspired additions, creating a classic du jour.

THE HOT DISH DEFINED

HOT DISH (FOOD): casserole-like food common in the Midwest; normally consists of a starch, a meat, and a vegetable mixed together with a sauce, often canned soup. —From *Dictionary of American Regional English*

Old Standby Hamburger and Rice Bake

This economical hot dish, my adaptation of an oldie called Texas Hash, appeared often on the table in the Nicollet Avenue apartment where I lived as a newlywed. I would hop off the bus and duck into the little corner grocery store to buy a pound of ground beef. The price? A now-unbelievable forty-three cents per pound. Up the stairs I'd go to my tiny kitchen on the third floor and pull the other ingredients from my cupboard.

While the casserole baked, I'd prepare the salad and set the table. My then-husband often read me tidbits out of the day's newspaper while I cooked. If I happened to have made a Jell-O salad—fruit or vegetables suspended in fruit-flavored gelatin was beloved in midcentury cooking—a day or two earlier, that shortened my work, allowing me to add a dessert.

A favorite quick salad was pear halves lined up in a 9-inch square and covered with lime-flavored gelatin (do this the night before). So easy to serve: Spread a lettuce leaf (always iceberg back then) on a salad plate, cut a portion of gelatin containing one pear half, lift the salad with a spatula and place it on the lettuce. A dollop of Miracle Whip could be added atop the pear. A speedy dessert, a favorite in those days, was chocolate instant pudding prepared with one cup milk and one cup sour cream. The sour cream lent a dark-chocolate tang to the simple dessert.

MAKES 6 SERVINGS

2 cups sliced onions or frozen chopped onion, thawed

1 cup chopped green or red pepper or frozen pepper stir-fry, thawed

2 tablespoons butter, margarine, or vegetable oil

¾ to 1 pound regular or lean ground beef

15-ounce can diced tomatoes or stewed tomatoes, chopped

4-ounce can chopped olives, drained (optional)

½ cup uncooked white rice

1 teaspoon chili powder

2 teaspoons salt

⅛ teaspoon pepper

Heat oven to 350° F.

Stir-fry onion and green pepper in butter until onions are yellow. Add meat and fry until meat is crumbled. Stir in tomatoes, olives, rice, chili powder, salt, and pepper. Turn mixture into sprayed or greased 2-quart casserole. Cover and bake 45 minutes; remove cover and return hash to oven for another 15 minutes.

 ## Cooks' Notes

Choose the type of ground beef that your family prefers and that fits your food budget. Regular ground beef, which contains 20 to 25 percent fat, is often used in dishes but the meat should be browned and drained of excess fat before mixing with other ingredients. Lean or extra lean ground beef (5 to 11 percent fat) is the choice when the meat will simpy be seasoned and shaped into patties, balls, or loaves, or added to a dish directly without first draining.

This mixture takes kindly to the addition of lurking leftovers, things such as peas, beans, or corn. Or shred a carrot and add it to the mix. That is, unless your family members are purists and refuse to eat an "enhanced" version.

Make-Ahead Lasagna

Everyone loves serving lasagna. What we don't love is boiling and handling those long, flat noodles—they tear so easily! So arrange your schedule so you can try this "cool" method. The morning of the day—or better yet, the night before—layer the uncooked noodles with all of the ingredients. Assemble the entire dish and refrigerate until you're ready to bake it. This allows time for the noodles to absorb the liquid, a process that will continue as the lasagna bakes. But don't rush the preparation: Give yourself enough time to layer the lasagna ingredients, distributing them evenly. This hearty dish has many variations—feel free to dream up your own.

MAKES 10 TO 12 SERVINGS

SAUCE

1 pound Italian sausage, pork sausage, or regular or lean ground beef

½ cup chopped onion (optional)

26-ounce bottle or can prepared spaghetti sauce

8 ounces tomato sauce, divided in half

RICOTTA MIXTURE

15 ounces fresh ricotta cheese or 2 cups cream-style cottage cheese

⅓ cup minced fresh parsley or 2 tablespoons parsley flakes

1 or 2 eggs, beaten

½ cup grated Parmesan or Romano cheese

¼ teaspoon pepper

TO COMPLETE LASAGNA

10 uncooked lasagne noodles (half of a 16-ounce package)

16 ounces shredded mozzarella cheese

1½ teaspoons anise seed

Grated Parmesan cheese for garnish (optional)

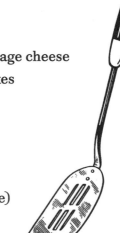

If using Italian sausage, remove meat from casings. Use a large skillet to cook sausage or beef and onion over medium heat until browned, 8 to 10 minutes. Drain off fat. Add spaghetti sauce and half of tomato sauce; mix well. In medium bowl, combine ricotta or cottage cheese, parsley, beaten egg(s), Parmesan or Romano, and pepper.

Spread remaining ⅓ cup tomato sauce on bottom of ungreased 9-by-13-inch baking dish. Top with 4 uncooked lasagne noodles. (I find it helpful to eyeball the portions of meat sauce, ricotta mixture, and mozzarella before layering. Spreading the layers with a rubber spatula works well.) Cover noodles with ⅓ of the meat sauce, then ½ of the ricotta mixture, and ⅓ of the shredded mozzarella. Repeat using 3 dry noodles, ⅓ of meat sauce, ½ the ricotta mixture, and another ⅓ of mozzarella. For final layer, use remaining 3 dry noodles, last ⅓ of meat sauce, and last ⅓ of mozzarella. Sprinkle with anise seed. Cover; refrigerate 8 hours or overnight.

When you're ready to bake the lasagna, heat oven to 375° F.

Bake covered 30 minutes. Remove cover and bake another 30 minutes, or until bubbly and heated through. Let stand 15 minutes before serving.

 Variations

Lasagna Roll-ups: Prepare meat sauce, ricotta mixture, and shredded cheese as above, except cook 12 noodles according to package directions. Spread the ½ cup tomato sauce in 9-by-13-inch baking dish. Lay out one noodle on a clean work surface. Spread about 4 tablespoons ricotta mixture down length of noodle—try dropping four 1-tablespoon dollops of mixture at intervals on pasta, then spreading with knife. Roll noodle up end to end. Place in prepared pan. Repeat with remaining noodles, arranging roll-ups in rows. Pour meat sauce generously over noodles—you may not need all of it. Cover meat sauce with thick layer of shredded cheese. Bake at 350° F about 35 minutes, or until bubbly. Makes 12 individual servings.

See recipe for White Lasagna with Beef on page 89.

Beef Stew the Oven Way (aka Football Stew)

This hearty and oh-so-easy dish is popular all over the Midwest, appearing in a number of versions with names that vary from Four-Hour Stew to Rest-Alot Stew. This version hails from Appleton, Wisconsin, where a group of forty-one close friends put together their stories and recipes in a book called *Foxy Ladies*. The stew is perfect for those fall football Sundays at the stadium or in front of the TV enjoying the excitement on the field, and then craving a stick-to-the-ribs supper. Or you might have this dish "stewing" in the oven while you're off for an afternoon of skating, skiing, or snowshoeing. It's so nice to come into a warm house and smell the meaty aroma. The "foxy ladies" recommend doubling or tripling the recipe, filling a large broiler pan while you're at it.

MAKES 4 SERVINGS

2 cups tomato juice*

2 tablespoons sugar

3 tablespoons minute tapioca

2 teaspoons salt

16 to 20 ounces beef stew meat

1 large onion, diced

4 carrots, peeled and sliced

1 rib celery, sliced

4 potatoes, peeled and cubed

*8-ounce can tomato sauce may be used; add water to make 2 cups.

Heat oven to 250° F.

In large bowl, stir together the tomato juice, sugar, tapioca, and salt. If chunks of stew meat are large, cut smaller. Mix meat (no need to brown), onion, carrots, celery, and potatoes in 3- to 4-quart casserole. Pour tomato juice mixture over stew ingredients; mix ingredients with two large spoons so meat and vegetables are coated with thickened tomato sauce.

Cover the baking dish with foil, sealing carefully. Bake stew for 4 hours until ingredients are fork tender.

 Variations

Speedy Beef Stew: Use 16-ounce bag frozen vegetables for stew to replace onion, carrots, celery, and potatoes.

Hunter's Stew: Use venison stew meat in place of beef.

Harvest-Time Stew: Replace 2 of the carrots with 2 parsnips, sliced. Or, substitute diced rutabaga for half of the potato. Or, simply add the parsnips and/or rutabaga to the stew for a more complex flavor.

Lamb Stew: Use cubed lamb shoulder in place of beef.

Chicken Pot Pie

Some folks love popping balloons. Kids think it's great to pop their bubble-gum bubbles. And everyone I know loves to take a fork and pop open the top of a pot pie. Tender, golden brown crust gives way to reveal creamy sauce dotted with chunks of chicken and colorful vegetables. This pie is quicker to make and easier to bake because it has one crust—the top—rather than the traditional two crusts.

MAKES 6 LARGE SERVINGS

FILLING
1 cup fresh or frozen peas
5 tablespoons butter, divided
3 tablespoons vegetable oil, divided
8 ounces mushrooms, sliced (3 cups or about 14 whole mushrooms before slicing)
2 carrots, peeled and thinly sliced
2 leeks, well washed and thinly sliced
12 chicken thighs, skinned, boned, and cut in 2-inch pieces
salt and pepper

CREAM SAUCE
2 tablespoons butter
3 tablespoons flour
1½ cups chicken broth
½ cup heavy (whipping) cream
¼ cup sliced green onions
3 tablespoons chopped fresh parsley or 1 tablespoon dried parsley flakes
1½ tablespoons chopped fresh tarragon (1½ teaspoons dried)

CRUST
Pastry for 10-inch single crust (recipe page 170)

Heat oven to 350° F.

Blanch (pour boiling water over) fresh peas for 2 minutes or thaw frozen ones. Drain and place peas in large mixing bowl. Melt 1 tablespoon of the butter with 1 tablespoon of the oil in large skillet. Add sliced mushrooms and stir-fry 5 minutes. Add mushrooms to peas. Put 4 tablespoons butter and 2 tablespoons oil in skillet. Add carrots and leeks; cover skillet. Cook over low heat 10 minutes, stirring now and then. Add to vegetable mixture. Season chicken with salt and pepper. Stir-fry in skillet 10 to 15 minutes until browned and almost done. Remove chicken mixture from skillet, add to vegetable mixture, and set aside.

For sauce: Add 2 tablespoons butter to skillet. Stir in flour. Cook until bubbly. Pour in chicken broth and cream. Simmer, stirring until thickened, about 5 minutes. Stir in onions, parsley, and tarragon. Mix cream sauce into chicken-vegetable mixture. Pour into greased square 2½-quart baking dish.

Top with unbaked pastry. Fold under edges of pastry to fit baking dish. Cut slashes in pastry to allow steam to escape. Bake 40 to 50 minutes, until pastry is browned and filling is bubbling.

 Variation

Chicken Pot Pie with Puff Pastry: Use 1 sheet thawed, frozen puff pastry in place of standard pastry crust.

The Best Turkey Wild Rice Hot Dish

Summer or winter, it's wonderful to roast a turkey over the weekend and enjoy the meat all week long in sandwiches, salads, and casseroles like this one. While oven roasting is typical, many cooks have a covered grill on their deck or balcony for use in cold weather. Today's turkeys roast quickly, so watch the meat thermometer or the pop-up thermometer in the bird.

Remember that roast turkey must go into the refrigerator as soon as you finish that first meal; it's highly perishable, so don't let it sit out while you chat.

MAKES 8 SERVINGS

⅓ cup chopped onion

⅓ cup chopped celery

⅓ cup chopped green pepper

8 ounces sliced fresh mushrooms*

½ cup butter

½ cup flour

1½ cups half-and-half**

1½ cups water

½ cup milk

4 cups cooked wild rice (see directions page 130) or 2 cups each cooked wild rice and brown rice

4 cups diced, cooked turkey

¼ cup diced pimento

1½ teaspoons salt

¼ teaspoon ground black pepper

⅓ cup slivered almonds

*or 6-ounce can broiled-in-butter-style sliced mushrooms
**or 12-ounce can low fat evaporated milk

Prepare wild rice ahead of time; see directions page 130.

Heat oven to 350° F.

In large saucepan, stir-fry onion, celery, green pepper, and mushrooms in butter until tender but not brown. Stir flour into vegetables and cook until flour bubbles. Gradually add half-and-half, water, and milk to vegetable mixture, stirring constantly until mixture boils. Cook and stir 1 minute longer, until thickened. Add wild rice, turkey, pimento, salt, and pepper.

Pour into greased 2½-quart baking dish. Sprinkle with almonds. Bake 40 to 50 minutes or until bubbling.

Menu Idea!

BUFFET SUPPER FOR A SPECIAL OCCASION

The Best Turkey Wild Rice Hot Dish

Ring of Jellied Cranberry Salad, Bowl of Mixed Green Salad

Whole Green Beans in Bundles with Pimento-Strip Ties

Bread Tray with a Seeded Crisp Bread,
a Sweet Bread, and a Corn Bread

Selection of Fruit Tarts or Fancy Cupcakes

Ladies-Who-Lunch Hot Salad

In the 1960s, which I recall as a more relaxed time before cell phones and multitasking, my friends and I each kept a little entertaining notebook. In it, we recorded the names of dishes we'd made for a particular occasion, describing how the food was served and received. My own notebook—ending with the menu for my daughter's first birthday party—even noted such personal details as my colleague Karen Sethre (now White) asking for milk for her coffee.

Another page reveals that on January 28, 1964, I served the tuna version of this salad for a supper for the director of the Betty Crocker Test Kitchens and the women who worked in Kamera Kitchen, all experts at preparing food for photography. These salads are ideal for bridge clubs, book groups, and showers.

MAKES 5 TO 6 SERVINGS

1 cup real mayonnaise (not salad dressing)

1 tablespoon lemon juice

¼ cup freshly grated Parmesan cheese

½ teaspoon salt

2 cups chopped cooked turkey or chicken

2 cups chopped celery

1 cup toasted bread cubes*

½ cup sliced water chestnuts (optional)

½ cup slivered almonds

¼ cup diced onion

Crushed Wheaties or corn flakes for topping

* Cut crusts from a slice of white or wheat bread, then cut bread into cubes and place on large baking sheet. With oven at 350° F, toast cubes until crisp.

Heat oven to 350° F.

In a small bowl, combine the mayonnaise, lemon juice, Parmesan cheese, and salt; mix well. Combine the turkey, celery, bread cubes, water chestnuts, almonds, and onion in a large mixing bowl; add mayonnaise mixture and toss well.

Put the mixture in a buttered casserole dish. Finish by sprinkling crushed cereal around the periphery of the dish. Bake uncovered about 40 minutes or until hot throughout.

 ## Variations

Individual Salads: Divide salad into individual ramekins; bake at 450° F for 12 to 15 minutes.

Hot Salad with Cheddar: Omit Parmesan cheese from mayonnaise mixture; sprinkle ½ cup grated Cheddar over salad before adding crushed cereal.

Hot Salad Gourmet: Use only 1 cup celery; instead add 1 cup chopped canned artichoke hearts, drained, or 9-ounce package frozen artichoke hearts, cooked, drained, and chopped.

A 1966 pamphlet, *Entertaining at Buffets, Teas and Parties,* published by the University of Minnesota and distributed via the homemakers' clubs of the Agricultural Extension Service, shares this advice:

 "Buffet service fits perfectly into our present informal way of life. If you are short of dining space and help, buffet service lets you entertain easily, yet graciously and pleasantly.

At the buffet table, a choice of foods is offered. Guests serve themselves, then eat in the living room or at small tables, according to the arrangements made by the hostess. Second servings are always in order. Part of the charm of the buffet is in the freedom your guests have to choose foods they like."

Tuna and Noodles

The ingredients for this well-loved combination are sure to be found in what we northerners call "the blizzard box," also known as "the emergency shelf" in other climes. This collection of canned and packaged foods can tide the family over when weather turns frightful, when you forget to thaw the meat, or even when money runs short. The tuna-pasta-sauce combination tastes mighty good, but it looks nondescript. So, long ago, a can of peas (later a package of frozen peas) was added, contributing color and vegetable nutrients. This version goes a step further by adding carrots to go with the peas, and cottage cheese to boost the protein. If you'd rather eat your carrots raw and your stash contains mushrooms, use a 4-ounce can of mushrooms stems and pieces, drained, in place of carrots.

MAKES 4 TO 6 SERVINGS

1½ cups uncooked egg noodles or macaroni (elbow, medium shell, or spiral)

2 tablespoons butter, margarine, or vegetable oil

¼ cup minced onion

2 ribs celery, sliced

3 tablespoons flour

¼ teaspoon salt

1½ cups milk

8 or 9 ounces frozen peas, rinsed

1 cup drained tuna (9½-ounce can)

1½ cups grated carrots

1 cup cottage cheese

1 tablespoon soy sauce

1 teaspoon salt

⅛ teaspoon black pepper

1 cup shredded Monterey Jack or Swiss cheese

Heat oven to 350° F.

Cook noodles or macaroni in boiling water according to package directions. Drain and set aside.

Melt butter in a large saucepan and stir-fry the onion and celery until onion is transparent. Stir the flour and ¼ teaspoon salt into ingredients in saucepan and cook until bubbly. Add milk gradually, cooking and stirring until the white sauce thickens. Remove the sauce from the heat. Stir in the drained pasta, peas, tuna, carrots, cottage cheese, and soy sauce. Taste and add the rest of salt and pepper. Pour the tuna mixture into a sprayed or buttered 2½-quart casserole.

Cover casserole with lid or with a sheet of foil and bake 35 to 40 minutes. Take off the cover and sprinkle on the shredded cheese. Bake 5 minutes or until cheese is melted.

 ## Variations

Chicken or Salmon and Noodles: Use 1½ cups diced leftover chicken or 1 to 1½ cups drained, canned salmon instead of tuna.

 ## Cooks' Notes

Prepare the hot dishes in this book with the milk that you keep on hand for drinking—whole, 2 percent, 1 percent, or skim. However, if a recipe specifies one type of milk—for example, the Easy Macaroni and Cheese calls for whole milk—be sure to use that milk because the eating quality of the finished dish depends on it. You may want to keep evaporated milk and nonfat dry milk powder on hand to use for cooking when you run out of fresh milk. Mix nonfat dry milk powder with water as directed on the package.

Easy Macaroni and Cheese

The Midwest—Wisconsin in particular—is famed for its dairy farms. Think gabled red barns; contented, mottled cows; and sturdy farmers squirting milk from the cow's teat into the mouth of the barn cat. But the dairy industry has had to deal with consumers' demand for foods lower in fat. Creameries, once central to rural towns, have closed as butter- and cheese-making and milk processing moved into factory settings. (Some creamery buildings have found new lives as restaurants and retail stores.) Now the dairy case is filled with low fat and no-fat products, still supplying important bone-building calcium. The late Ruth Brand developed this stir-and-bake mac and cheese when she worked at the Dairy Council in St. Paul. Her daughter Alice Brand Hawks, a former editor of the Betty Crocker Cookbooks, gave it to me.

MAKES 6 SERVINGS

¼ cup butter

2⅓ cups uncooked elbow macaroni (7-ounce package)

2 cups grated sharp Cheddar cheese or cubed American cheese (8 ounces)

3 tablespoons flour

1 quart whole milk

½ teaspoon salt

⅛ teaspoon pepper

Heat oven to 325° F.

Melt butter in medium pan. Pour half the butter into 2½-quart baking dish. Pour in macaroni and stir until butter coats macaroni thoroughly. Sprinkle cheese over macaroni. Stir flour into remaining 2 tablespoons butter and cook until forming a paste. Pour milk into pan; add salt and pepper. Cook and stir until milk is hot. Pour milk mixture over macaroni in dish.

Bake uncovered 1 hour, until macaroni is tender and coated with sauce.

 **Variations**

Mac and Cheese with Ham or SPAM: Add 1 cup diced baked ham or browned, diced SPAM luncheon meat with cheese.

Veggie Mac and Cheese: Add 1 to 2 cups of any combination of cooked left-over vegetables.

Menu Idea!

FOR-OLD-TIMES-SAKE LUNCH

Easy Macaroni and Cheese

Stewed Tomatoes

Plate of Carrot and Celery Sticks

Small Bowl of Pimento-Stuffed Olives

Applesauce

Oatmeal Raisin Cookies

Take-Your-Choice Strata

What to cook when there's nothing to cook? Strata is one answer. Most kitchens are stocked with bread, milk, and eggs. Find some cheese and you're all set. Variations are limited only by the contents of your pantry and your imagination. The strata bakes up lighter and fluffier if you can refrigerate it for a time before baking, but it's not a must. These directions call for making the layers sandwich style in a square pan, but you can use a round casserole by slicing the buttered bread into quarters or cubes, then making two or three layers according to the depth of your dish. Tuna Sandwich Casserole, featured in a North Dakota community cookbook, inspired this version. My daughter Barb, who is my official taster, and I found the strata made with ham and broccoli every bit as good the second day.

MAKES 3 TO 4 SERVINGS

4 slices bread, buttered one side and cut in half, divided*

1 to 1½ cups grated or shredded cheese, divided

¾ to 1 cup chopped vegetables, fresh or frozen (optional)

½ to 1 cup diced meat (leftover roast beef, pork, chicken, or canned meat or fish, optional)

2 eggs, well beaten

1½ cups milk (use part half-and-half for a richer dish)

½ teaspoon dry mustard

*cut off crusts if necessary to make bread fit pan

Arrange 4 half slices of bread to fill bottom of buttered 8-inch square pan. Sprinkle bread with half the cheese. Top cheese with a vegetable or two—I suggest frozen chopped broccoli, cut green beans, cut asparagus, chopped spinach, or mixed vegetables. Also good: shredded carrot, finely chopped celery, or a tablespoon or two of minced onion. Atop vegetables, add leftover cooked meat or a canned meat or fish, if you have some. Possible protein additions: tuna, salmon, or shrimp; diced sandwich meats such as honey ham; leftover roast beef, pork, or chicken.

Cover all with the remaining 4 buttered half slices of bread. Distribute remaining cheese evenly over bread. Beat together eggs, milk, and dry mustard and pour over layers. Cover and refrigerate until ready to bake.

Bake in preheated oven at 325° F for 40 to 45 minutes, until puffed and golden and you can smell the cheese.

 **Variations**

Loaf Pan Strata: Use whole bread slices; fit them closely into buttered 9-inch loaf pan.

Big Batch Strata: Use a 9-by-13-inch pan and double all ingredients.

After Easter Strata: Use 1 to 1½ cups diced baked ham and 1 to 1½ cut cooked asparagus or broccoli.

Scalloped Potatoes

Most cooks don't need a recipe for this beloved potato preparation. They simply peel and slice the potatoes, then arrange them in the casserole adding dots of butter and generous sprinklings of flour, salt, and pepper between the layers. Pour on hot milk and into the oven it goes alongside the meat for that evening's meal. I'm told scalloped potatoes with baked ham or meatballs is the main dish of choice for funerals in South Dakota. Knowing that peeling potatoes was a much-disliked chore, makers of convenience foods developed mixes for both scalloped and au gratin potatoes. These mixes will do in a pinch, but when you taste this casserole side by side with one prepared from a mix, I think you'll agree that the dish made with fresh potatoes has a cleaner and more distinct flavor. Hats off to Jeanette Tieberg, Virginia, Minnesota, who shared this garlic-fragrant version in *Simply Delicious: Herberger's Employee Family Recipes.*

MAKES 4 SERVINGS

About 4 cups peeled, sliced potatoes (2 large or 4 medium)
¼ cup minced onion
¼ cup chopped fresh parsley
1 cup shredded Cheddar cheese
2 tablespoons butter or margarine
1 clove garlic, minced
1½ cups milk
1½ tablespoons cornstarch
½ teaspoon salt
⅛ teaspoon pepper

Heat oven to 350° F.

Arrange half the potatoes in a buttered 2-quart casserole. Top with half the onion, parsley, and cheese. Make a second layer of potatoes, onion, parsley, and cheese. Melt butter and stir-fry garlic in medium saucepan 1 minute or until you smell the garlic. Blend milk, cornstarch, salt, and pepper in medium bowl. Pour milk mixture into saucepan with garlic; cook and stir until thickened. Pour over potatoes.

Bake for 1 hour or until potatoes are tender when tested with a two-tined kitchen fork.

 Variations

Ham and Scalloped Potatoes: Use 1 to 2 cups diced baked ham in place of cheese.

Old-Time Scalloped Potatoes: Omit cheese in Scalloped Potatoes recipe.

Meatballs and Scalloped Potatoes: Arrange 1 to 2 cups thawed frozen meatballs between the two layers of potatoes—omit cheese.

 Cooks' Notes

Scalloped potatoes can be baked at temperatures as low as 300° F in order to share the oven with a roast; increase baking time to compensate for lower temperature.

Farmers' Market Corn Pudding

Happy the cook who has a lively farmers' market nearby. A generation ago we stopped at a favorite farm stand on the way home to buy vegetables—and sometimes eggs and honey. Now most communities have outdoor markets where fresh-from-the-field vegetables are piled on the tables. Early in the spring these markets sell bedding plants; a bit later asparagus arrives. As the season advances, vendors offer berries, corn (for casseroles like this one), tomatoes, cukes, peppers, and finally melons and squash. Sometimes an enterprising farm wife will market jam or fruit-filled baked goods. I love to chat with the farmers as I look over the offerings.

In Minnesota, hundreds of Hmong from Laos are farming; they market Asian vegetables, such as long beans and daikon radishes. Alongside the vegetables and herbs, women offer their distinctive storytelling embroideries.

Farmers markets work well for singles like myself because you can bargain for the amount you need, one green pepper, one eggplant, and so on. As a townhouse dweller with no flower garden, I can take home a pretty bouquet, too.

MAKES 4 TO 6 SERVINGS

3 eggs

½ cup milk

½ cup half-and-half or 5-ounce can fat-free evaporated milk

2 cups drained whole kernel corn (canned or frozen or cooked fresh)

1 tablespoon grated onion or 2 tablespoons sliced green onion

½ teaspoon salt

Freshly ground pepper to taste

2 tablespoons fine cracker crumbs (optional)

Heat oven to 350° F (325° for a glass dish).

Select a 1-quart baking dish and a slightly larger pan that can hold the dish and about one inch of water. In medium bowl, beat together eggs, milk, and half-and-half. Stir in drained corn, onion, salt, and pepper. Pour into 1-quart baking dish. Sprinkle crumbs on top.

To bake pudding in water bath, place baking dish in the large pan. Using both hands, carefully lift both pans and place in the oven. Pour hot tap water into large pan, about 1 inch deep. Bake 50 to 60 minutes or until knife inserted 1 inch from edge comes out clean.

 **Variations**

Carrot Pudding: Use 2 cups sliced cooked carrots in place of corn; omit crumbs.

Carrot Timbales: Divide Carrot Pudding mixture among 8 custard cups or ramekins, baking 20 to 25 minutes.

Round the World in a Casserole Dish

Satisfying Shepherd's Pie

Moussaka

Hungarian Goulash Casserole

Tourtiere

Cassoulet

Arroz con Pollo

Diana's Moctezuma Pie

Afghani Chicken Bake

Cauliflower Cheese

Tian of Zucchini, Rice, and Cheese

COOKING AND EATING DISHES FROM OTHER COUNTRIES offers two advantages: First, we can discover new flavors and ingredients from our multicultural world. Second, we can recall wonderful eating experiences from the past, either from travel or time spent in another country.

Minnesota food writer and wild rice expert Beth Anderson coined the phrase "table traveling" to describe getting acquainted with a distant land via its food. Beth has advocated traveling via the family table in the columns of "Taste," the *Minneapolis Star Tribune*'s food section. In geography or foreign language classes, linking the study of a faraway place with its food is natural. Students can both study a culture *and* learn about it by helping to prepare its food. The recipes that I've developed after tasting a new dish while traveling are unique souvenirs.

Happily, enjoying exotic, ethnic flavors has become much easier as our planet evolves into a global village. Thanks to air cargo and huge refrigerated ships, we in the Midwest can enjoy produce grown in sunny Central and South America in midwinter.

So, spin the globe, pick a region, and get busy on the Internet finding recipes from exotic places. The recipes that follow only scratch the surface of the wealth of table-travel experiences awaiting you.

Satisfying Shepherd's Pie

On her first trip to Great Britain at seventeen, my daughter Barb fell in love with shepherd's pie, which we tasted several times as we traveled first to London, then to Edinburgh, Scotland, and Waterford, Ireland, where we visited her two pen pals. We tracked down this recipe and she's been making it ever since. On a later trip to Ireland, she learned to make a terrific trifle: pound cake soaked with sherry, then layered with raspberry preserves and vanilla pudding, and, finally, topped with clouds of sweetened whipped cream. It has become our traditional Christmas Day dessert.

MAKES 4 SERVINGS

2 tablespoons vegetable oil

1 cup chopped onion (1 large)

1 clove garlic, minced or finely chopped

1 pound regular or lean ground beef

1 large carrot, grated, or 15-ounce can sliced carrots or mixed peas and carrots, drained

1 tablespoon fresh thyme leaves or 1 teaspoon dried thyme

1½ to 2 tablespoons Worcestershire sauce

Few grinds black pepper

3 cups mashed potatoes (leftover homemade, thawed frozen, or prepared from an instant mix)

Heat oven to 375° F.

Heat oil in a large, heavy skillet. Add onion and garlic; stir-fry until onion is translucent. Add ground beef, breaking it into chunks. Brown beef for a few minutes, then add carrots and thyme. Cook 5 minutes more. Stir in Worcestershire sauce and pepper. Spoon meat mixture into a 10-inch pie plate or 8-inch round baking dish. Spoon mashed potatoes on top of meat mixture, making an even layer. Use the back of a tablespoon to make swirls in the potatoes.

Bake 25 to 30 minutes or until meat mixture bubbles and potatoes are golden.

 ## Variations

Monday-or-Tuesday Shepherd's Pie: Use 2 cups finely diced leftover roast beef in place of ground beef.

Friday Shepherd's Pie: Use 16-ounce can salmon, drained, in place of beef.

Menu Idea!

SUPPER WITH A BRITISH ACCENT
Satisfying Shepherd's Pie

Steamed Cauliflower, Brussels Sprouts, or Cabbage

Bread and Butter

Fresh Berries with Heavy Cream

Moussaka

This is the national dish of Greece, satisfying to soul and body. I got this recipe from Margaret Maunder, a fellow writer now living in Connecticut. Margaret had been introduced to moussaka by a Greek student who served it for Thanksgiving dinner. Says Margaret: "I discovered that moussaka ranks close to the Acropolis as a contribution to civilization. Who needed turkey!"

I enjoyed moussaka often when vacationing in the Greek Islands twenty years ago. Typically, when you go into a taverna for a meal, the host simply invites you to visit the kitchen to peer into the pots on the stove and select your main dish and vegetables. No language barrier—you just point.

MAKES 6 SERVINGS

2 pounds boiling potatoes

2 onions, minced

2 cloves garlic, minced

2 tablespoons vegetable oil, preferably olive oil

1 pound regular or lean ground beef

½ teaspoon nutmeg

½ teaspoon cinnamon

Salt and pepper to taste

6-ounce can tomato paste mixed with ¾ cup water

2 eggs

1⅛ cups milk

½ cup grated Parmesan cheese

Heat oven to 375° F.

Boil potatoes in their skins in salted water 30 minutes. Cool, peel, and slice ¼-inch thick. Stir-fry onion and garlic in oil in large skillet. Add meat and seasonings. Brown the meat 10 minutes. Drain off excess fat. Add tomato mixture; simmer 10 minutes.

Grease a 13-by-9-inch baking dish. Arrange half of potato slices in dish. Spread meat mixture evenly over potatoes. Spread rest of potatoes over meat layer. Beat eggs and milk with a little salt. Pour over layered ingredients. Sprinkle top with cheese.

Bake uncovered 40 minutes, or until golden brown. Remove from oven and let stand 10 minutes before cutting. Serve in squares.

 **Variation**

Moussaka with Eggplant: Use sliced eggplant in place of potatoes, frying eggplant quickly in oil before layering in baking dish.

 Menu Idea!

GREEK ISLE SUPPER
Salad of Tomato and Cucumber Chunks with Feta Cheese

Moussaka

Crusty Peasant-Style Bread

Plain Yogurt with Honey for Dessert

Thick, Dark, Strong Coffee

Hungarian Goulash Casserole

Movie producer Joseph Pasternak left his native Hungary to live and work in this country, but he never forgot the distinctive dishes of his native land, which he called "the land of glamorous women and gypsy violins." In the introduction to his anecdote-filled cookbook, he wrote: "In my native land and in other countries of the continent where I have lived, loved and cooked, I learned that the basic ingredient in good cooking is love—love of good food and love of the good people you cook for." Little wonder he named the book *Cooking with Love and Paprika*. Here is the dish he prepared for his publisher in order to prove he knew his way around the kitchen.

MAKES 6 TO 8 SERVINGS

2 pounds pork leg or shoulder

3 tablespoons flour

2 teaspoons salt

1 teaspoon sweet Hungarian paprika

¼ teaspoon cayenne pepper

1 medium onion, minced

1 clove garlic, minced

1 green pepper, chopped

1 large tomato, peeled and chopped

2 tablespoons vegetable oil, shortening, or butter

4 to 5 tablespoons water, more as needed

15-ounce can sauerkraut, drained

1 pint sour cream

Dash of caraway seeds

Dice the meat into bite-size pieces. Mix the flour, salt, paprika, and cayenne pepper together in a paper bag. Shake the meat in the paper bag to coat well on all sides. Then stir-fry the meat with the onion, garlic, green pepper, and tomato in oil until golden. Add water, cover, and simmer until the meat is tender, about 1½ hours. Check during cooking and, if necessary, add a little more water.

Rinse the sauerkraut and drain again. Start heating oven to 350° F. Mix kraut into the meat. Add the sour cream, caraway seeds, and a little more water; stir well. Place in a 2½-quart casserole dish.

Bake uncovered for 30 minutes. Taste and correct seasoning before serving. Serve with boiled potatoes.

Menu Idea!

RECALLING BUDAPEST

Hungarian Goulash Casserole

Sliced Cucumbers with Sour Cream Dressing

Hearty Rye Bread

Very Thin Pancakes folded in quarters

with Warm Chocolate Sauce

Tourtiere

Our neighbors in French Canada traditionally serve this fragrant meat pie following midnight mass on Christmas Eve. Now that there's ready-to-bake pie crust in the refrigerated case at the supermarket, this delicious dish need not be reserved for the holidays. It's excellent any time the weather is cold or raw. Some versions thicken the meat with potato, but rolled oats are quicker to use and equally authentic.

MAKES 6 SERVINGS

1 pound lean ground pork

¾ cup water

1 medium onion, chopped (1 cup)

1 clove garlic, minced (optional)

½ cup finely chopped celery (2 ribs)

1 bay leaf

1 teaspoon ground thyme or savory

¼ teaspoon ground black pepper

¼ teaspoon dried rosemary

¼ teaspoon grated nutmeg

pinch of cinnamon

1 teaspoon salt or to taste

½ cup old fashioned rolled oats

Pastry for double crust pie (recipe page 170, your favorite recipe, or refrigerated premade pastry rounds)

Heat oven to 375° F.

Crumble pork into a large, heavy skillet. Add water and bring to a boil. Add onion, garlic, celery, bay leaf, thyme, pepper, rosemary, nutmeg, and cinnamon. Cover skillet and cook over medium-low heat 1 hour. After 30 minutes, check to see whether a little more water is needed; if so, add water. Stir in salt. When meat is done, remove bay leaf and stir in rolled oats. Cook, stirring 1 to 2 minutes. Set this meat filling aside to cool.

Meanwhile, line a 9- to 10-inch pie plate (preferably glass) with 1 round of pastry. When filling is lukewarm, heat oven to 350° F. Spoon pork filling into pie shell. Top with second pastry round. Press the edges of the top and bottom crusts together, tucking the top one over the bottom one to make a thick edge. Crimp the edges with the tines of a fork or use thumb and forefinger to flute them. Cut vents or a simple design into the top crust so steam can escape while pie is baking.

Bake 25 to 35 minutes or until crust is golden; you'll be able to smell the spicy pork aroma. If desired, pass a bowl of Mushroom Sauce (Cream Sauce [1 cup, recipe page 168] heated with 4-ounce can mushrooms, drained) or Tomato Sauce (heated canned tomato sauce with a dash of dried basil) to ladle over Tourtiere.

Cassoulet

The cassoulet has been called the archetypal peasant meal. This cassoulet is a modern take on the time-honored French version, which was cooked in two stages: first the beans simmered with the vegetables and herbs in a low oven; then after adding the meats, it cooked in a medium oven.

I think of cassoulet as the culinary ancestor of today's bean casseroles such as Cowboy Beans (recipe page 94). Bean-rich dishes like this are healthy as well. Medical research shows that eating beans regularly—in soups, casseroles, and salads—is beneficial for one's cholesterol. What's more, bean dishes with a small amount of meat complement the protein in the beans. One more thing: for optimum nutrition, serve a bean entrée and a citrus fruit in the same meal.

MAKES 6 SERVINGS

5 to 6 cups cooked navy beans or other small white beans (1 pound dry or three 15-ounce cans, drained)

2 tablespoons olive or vegetable oil

⅔ cup chopped onion

2 cloves garlic, minced

½ pound pork loin, cut in 1-inch cubes

1¼ pounds boneless chicken, cut in 1-inch cubes

1 cup chicken broth

1 cup tomato sauce

¼ cup white wine

1 tablespoon minced fresh thyme or ½ teaspoon dried leaf thyme

1 bay leaf

½ pound smoked sausage, cut in 1-inch-thick slices

2 teaspoons dried parsley or 2 tablespoons minced fresh parsley

⅓ cup fine bread crumbs

Heat oven to 350° F.

Place drained beans in a 2½-quart baking dish. Heat oil in large, heavy skillet and stir-fry onion and garlic until soft. Add pork and chicken cubes to skillet and brown lightly. Stir together the chicken broth, tomato sauce, wine, thyme, and bay leaf in a separate bowl. Add sausage slices and onion-meat mixture to beans in baking dish and mix well. Then pour in broth-herb mixture, add parsley and mix again.

Bake covered for 1 hour.

Stir contents gently. Sprinkle bread crumbs over top of casserole and bake uncovered 20 minutes longer, until crumbs are nicely browned. Serve in bowls or on plates. Be sure to serve crusty French bread for sopping up the flavorful juices.

 **Variations**

Lamb Cassoulet: Use 1 pound lamb stew meat, cut in cubes, in place of chicken.

Not-So-Beany Cassoulet: Use 2 cups diced cooked tomatoes or carrots in place of 2 cups of the beans.

Arroz con Pollo

From Spain comes this wonderful potluck or buffet dish; the name means Rice with Chicken. It is adapted from *Galley Ho: A Collection of Writers' Recipes*, published in 1967 by the Twin Cities chapter of what is now the Association for Women in Communications.

MAKES 8 SERVINGS

1 pound each chicken breasts and legs

2 pounds chicken thighs

2 cups uncooked white rice

¼ cup butter

¼ cup olive or vegetable oil

1 small onion, chopped (⅓ cup)

2 cloves garlic, pressed or minced

4-ounce can mushroom stems and pieces, drained,
or 8 ounces sliced fresh mushrooms (about 3 cups or 14 whole)

1 green pepper, chopped

½ cup dry sherry

4 cups chicken broth

2 teaspoons salt

¼ teaspoon rosemary

3 large tomatoes, peeled and chopped (about 2 cups),
or 1 cup diced canned tomatoes

2 tablespoons grated Parmesan or Romano cheese

1 fresh red pepper or 2 canned roasted red peppers, cut in strips

Ahead of time: Poach chicken parts (cook gently in water or chicken broth until tender). Remove chicken meat from bones, leaving it in good-sized chunks. Cover and refrigerate until needed.

Heat oven to 350° F.

Wash rice thoroughly; dry as much as possible. Melt butter with oil in large skillet. Stir-fry rice, onion, and garlic in butter mixture until golden brown. Add mushrooms and green pepper and stir-fry 4 to 5 minutes. Add sherry, chicken broth, salt, rosemary, and tomatoes. Bring to a boil, stirring constantly. Transfer mixture to a 2-quart casserole. Bake 20 minutes.

Remove casserole from oven and lower oven to 325° F. Stir and add chunks of chicken. Sprinkle with cheese and decorate with red pepper. Cover casserole. Bake 30 minutes or until rice is done and all liquid is absorbed.

Menu Idea!

SUPPER ESPAÑOL

Arroz con Pollo

Relish Tray of Olives and Marinated Vegetables

Crusty Rolls

Vanilla Ice Cream with Sherried Orange Segments
drizzled with Caramel Sauce

Diana's Moctezuma Pie

Diana Kennedy, the woman who almost single-handedly put Mexican cooking on the American culinary map, featured this recipe in *The Essential Cuisines of Mexico*. She describes Moctezuma pie as "rather solid and luscious, and certainly not recommended for calorie counters." The pie is named for the last Aztec emperor in Mexico; he was overthrown by Spanish conquistadors.

MAKES 4 SERVINGS

TOMATO SAUCE

15-ounce can diced tomatoes

2 cloves garlic, peeled

½ teaspoon salt

¼ teaspoon sugar

½ cup water

GREEN SAUCE

2 (4-ounce) cans peeled green chilies

½ medium onion, sliced

¼ teaspoon salt

3 tablespoons vegetable oil

PIE

⅓ cup vegetable oil

12 corn tortillas (6-inch or 7-inch size), cut in half

2 cups shredded cooked chicken or turkey

1½ cups sour cream

1¾ cups grated Cheddar cheese

Heat oven to 350° F.

Prepare tomato sauce by mixing the tomatoes, garlic, salt, sugar, and water in blender. Cook mixture in two tablespoons oil over high heat about 8 minutes, until thickened. Set aside. Follow the same method to prepare the green sauce, blending the chilies, sliced onion, and salt and cooking the sauce in oil.

Heat the ⅓ cup oil and fry each tortilla half a few seconds—they should not get crisp or hard. Kitchen tongs work well for handling tortillas. Drain tortillas on paper towel. Arrange 8 of the tortilla halves in the bottom of a deep 2½-quart round baking dish. Layer on top of tortillas half the chicken, half the green sauce, and ⅓ each of the tomato sauce, sour cream, and cheese. Repeat the layers, finishing with a layer of tortilla halves; cover with the rest of the sauce, sour cream, and cheese.

Bake 25 minutes, or until pie is bubbling. The tortillas on the bottom should be soft and those on top still chewy.

MEXICO MEANS COLOR IN FRUITS—AND FLOWERS

Our neighbors south of the border enjoy nature's vibrant colors all year round. Plants there don't freeze back, so they grow and grow. Poinsettia plants become bushes loaded with the red blossoms we prize at holiday time. Bougainvillea vines work their way up walls and across roofs, flashing red and purple. The busy *mercados* or markets feature tables heaped with produce: glistening green avocados (so big a half is a whole meal), glowing orange papaya, fat red and green peppers, golden pineapples and lemons as big as our oranges. In the spice section, you can take your choice of herbs and chilies—fresh, dried, or ground—so fragrant, so enticing.

Afghani Chicken Bake

In the mid-1970s, Afghanistan-born Abdul Kayoum came to St. Paul, Minnesota, and opened a restaurant called Caravan Serai. The ambiance was exotic with tent-like ceilings and, in one room, low tables surrounded by pillows to sit on. And the fare was delectable. Abby, as he was called by aficionados like my then-editor, the late Bill Greer, delighted in introducing midwesterners to his native land's specialties. I recall that the lentil soup had yogurt in it, a food we were just then getting to know. And the chicken was cooked with apricots . . . mmm. Abby's daughter Nancy now runs the Caravan Serai, though in a different location. Later, Asad Gharwal, another Afghan expatriate, started Da Afghan in Bloomington, Minnesota, also introducing the foodways of the Afghan people. Capitalizing on our interest in healthy recipes, he published *Award Winning Low-Fat Afghani Cooking* in 1995. After I served this recipe from Gharwal's book, my home was redolent of garlic for two days.

Garlic has always been a favorite ingredient of mine. Now that it's proven to be one of the healthiest foods you can eat, I serve it even more often. For the greatest amount of flavor and nutrition, I recommend using fresh garlic, not the bottled kind or the granulated version. Investing in a good garlic press will make cooking with fresh garlic a snap.

MAKES 4 SERVINGS

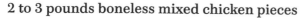

2 to 3 pounds boneless mixed chicken pieces

1 tablespoon corn oil

3 medium potatoes, peeled and chunked

3 medium carrots, peeled and chunked

1 tomato, sliced

1 green pepper, sliced

TOMATO SAUCE

6-ounce can tomato paste

1¾ cups water

1 tablespoon crushed garlic

1 teaspoon salt

1 teaspoon freshly ground coriander seeds

1 teaspoon black pepper

¼ teaspoon cayenne pepper

Hot cooked white rice, preferably basmati

Heat oven to 375° F. Wash chicken, removing skin and fat; if chicken breasts are large, cut in half. Heat oil in a large frying pan over medium heat and brown chicken.

Cut potatoes and carrots in large pieces. In a 2½-quart greased baking dish, layer the chicken, sliced tomato, sliced green pepper, potatoes, and carrots. Combine ingredients for tomato sauce and pour over chicken in baking dish.

Cover and bake for 1 hour or until chicken and potatoes are tender when pierced with a kitchen fork. Serve with mounds of rice to soak up the garlicky tomato sauce.

Cauliflower Cheese

Many an evening you'll find me curled up in my big chair reading a novel. My favorites are written by English authors, among them Rosamunde Pilcher and Joanna Trollope. The main characters in their books are often attractive young mothers who like to put together a dish of cauliflower cheese, drive off in their minis to do their errands, and frequently pause for a restoring cup of black tea. Those casseroles of cheese-topped cauliflower sounded so satisfying that I just had to learn how to make them.

MAKES 4 SERVINGS

1 medium cauliflower, divided into florets (about 5 cups)

2 tablespoons butter

3 tablespoons flour

1 teaspoon salt

1½ cups milk

1 cup grated Cheddar cheese (4 ounces)

Dash of cayenne pepper

2 tablespoons prepared bread crumbs

Heat oven to 400° F.

Boil the cauliflower in salted water 10 minutes, until almost tender. Or, if pre-ferred, cook cauliflorets in microwave in ½ cup water in 1½-quart baking dish, covered, on High for 7 to 9 minutes. Drain cauliflower thoroughly. Place cauli-florets in buttered 1½-quart baking dish.

To prepare the sauce: melt the butter in a saucepan, stir in the flour and salt, and then add the milk gradually. Stir in ¾ cup grated cheese and cayenne pep-per. Cook 2 minutes, stirring frequently until thickened. Pour the sauce over the cauliflower. Sprinkle with remaining cheese and bread crumbs.

Place in hot oven for 5 minutes. Remove from oven and turn heat to broil. Broil casserole 3 minutes to brown the cheese and crumbs.

 **Variations**

Broccoli Cheese: Use 5 cups cut-up fresh broccoli in place of cauliflower. If you want to use the broccoli stems, peel them before dicing them.

Cheese-Topped Mixed Vegetables: Use 5 cups frozen California-mix veg-etables (cauliflower, broccoli, and carrots) in place of fresh cauliflower. Cook vegetables according to package directions.

Tian of Zucchini, Rice, and Cheese

The bumper crops of late summer zucchini squash in the Midwest are both a standing joke and a cook's challenge. Recipes using the small or medium squash before they become giant-size are much in demand. I found this wonderful zucchini recipe from Italy in *The World of Cheese*, an international guide to cheeses with a fine collection of recipes. The author, Minnesota-reared Evan Jones, also wrote the definitive *American Food: The Gastronomic Story*, marking the bicentennial in 1976. Oh, yes, tian is another name for casserole.

MAKES 4 SERVINGS

4 small or 3 medium zucchini squash

1 tablespoon coarse salt

3 tablespoons butter

4 green onions, chopped

1 small clove garlic, whole

½ to ¾ cup heavy cream or combination of sour and heavy cream

1¼ cups grated mild, semisoft cheese, such as Bel Paese, Fontina, or Monterey Jack

2 cups cooked white or brown rice

salt and freshly ground pepper

2 tablespoons chopped fresh parsley and basil

2 tablespoons fresh bread crumbs

1 tablespoon grated hard cheese, such as Parmesan

Trim the zucchini and grate it coarsely. Toss with salt and let sit in a colander to drain for about 30 minutes; squeeze dry.

Heat oven to broil.

Heat butter in skillet and stir-fry grated zucchini with the green onions about 5 minutes. Add a very small amount of garlic to skillet by using a knife to scrape some of the juice from a small clove. Add cream and simmer another 5 minutes or so. Next fold in the grated cheese, cooked rice, and salt and pepper to taste. Continue heating and add the herbs. Turn mixture into a buttered shallow round casserole (the tian). Mix bread crumbs and grated cheese, sprinkle over top.

Brown under broiler until cheese melts and mixture is bubbling hot.

Menu Idea!

WHEN IN ROME

Melon Slices Wrapped in Prosciutto Ham

Sole or Bass Filets Fried in Garlicky Oil

Tian of Zucchini, Rice, and Cheese

Crisp Bread Sticks

Sugared Grape Clusters

Biscotti

Comfort Foods for Busy Days

Shipwreck Casserole

Tater Tot Hot Dish

Biscuit-Topped Beef and Vegetable Casserole

Meat 'n' Potatoes Hot Dish

The Cedric Adams Hot Dish

Corned Beef Casserole

Pizza Rice

Norte-Americano Tamale Pie

Cabbage and Sausage Supper

Ham-Broccoli Bake

Chicken with Rice and Two Soups

Salmon Supreme

Green and Gold Casserole

RESTAURATEURS DISCOVER comfort foods every other year, it seems. But home cooks have never forgotten how soothing a batch of macaroni and cheese or a bowl of rice custard can be when someone in the household is sad or stressed. Food magazines may feature the new, the trendy, and the elegant. But when it comes right down to it, something creamy, bubbly, and with a rich aroma—and just out of the oven—is sure to brighten the eyes of those around the table.

SIMPLICITY AND SOPHISTICATION

Many credit the late Marian Tracy with starting the casserole craze when she wrote *Casserole Cookery: One-dish meals for the lazy gourmet* (New York: Modern Age) in 1941. War brides and women working outside the home for the first time loved her simple recipes and told their friends about them. Here's part of her introduction:

"Being lazy and liking to cook and to entertain, we [husband and co-author Nino] struggled futilely for a long time over how to combine these features pleasantly. Finally the thing came to us—that thing being a casserole. Stews and other wrongly demeaned dishes take on a dash of simplicity and sophistication when prepared in a casserole. Essentially a one-dish meal, it requires little watching, a side serving of some green salad, bread, and your preference of drink. We can come home late, put a casserole in the oven, and relax—a unique indulgence. Our motto is: Pamper self and stomach, but let the food take care of itself."

Shipwreck Casserole

This unusual name caught my eye when scanning church and community cookbooks loaned to me by educator Geri Bosch, who hails from Ashley, North Dakota, and by retired nursing home administrator Caryl Crozier, who grew up in Beresford, South Dakota. After trying the recipe and liking it, I checked various sources, finding many slightly different versions. Other names for this popular combo are Busy Day Casserole and Seven-Layer Casserole (made without carrots or celery). I would dearly love to know where the name Shipwreck comes from; I can only surmise that it's a dish families turn to when life has "shipwrecked" and they need something easy and familiar.

MAKES 4 TO 6 SERVINGS

1 medium onion, chopped or thin sliced

2 to 3 medium potatoes, diced, grated, or thin sliced

2 carrots, grated or thin sliced

1 pound regular or lean ground beef or turkey, raw, crumbled

⅓ cup uncooked white or brown rice

1 to 2 ribs celery, sliced

1 can red kidney beans, drained and rinsed

Salt and pepper to taste

1 can tomato soup

1 cup water

Heat oven to 350° F (325° F for glass casserole).

Layer the vegetables, meat, rice, and beans in the order given in a 2-quart casserole, seasoning each layer lightly with salt and a dash of pepper. Stir soup and water together and pour over the layered ingredients.

Cover and bake 1½ hours. Use a kitchen fork to test vegetables for doneness.

LET'S DO SOME DOVETAILING

As future home economists (not to mention homemakers), my Iowa State classmates and I were taught "dovetailing." To dovetail is to carry out one task within another, as closely as one feather fits next to the other in a dove's tail. One example: reorganize one kitchen drawer each afternoon while dinner is cooking, doing this each day until all the drawers have had a going-over. Another idea: Keep a box of note cards and stamps in the kitchen so you can jot notes to friends and relatives yet keep an eye on what's simmering or baking. Dovetailing was, of course, the forerunner of today's multitasking.

Tater Tot Hot Dish

This is another of those hot dishes that is adapted and adjusted by every cook who regularly makes it. Some top the meat layer with grated cheese. Others mix canned mushrooms with the vegetable layer. And there's a version called Bachelor's Tater Tot Hot Dish. You double the recipe below using 2 pounds of meat and the full 16-ounce bag of frozen veggies. To fit all the Tater Tots from the 2-pound bag, you need to place them on end rather than sideways. Even then, they probably won't all fit. Presumably, the bachelor would scoop out a portion each day and warm it up for a quick, filling supper.

MAKES 4 SERVINGS

1 pound regular or lean ground beef or ground turkey

1 onion, chopped (½ cup)

2 cups (8 ounces) frozen vegetables of your choice, such as peas and carrots or mixed vegetables

10-ounce can cream of chicken or cream of mushroom soup

½ cup milk

16 ounces frozen Tater Tots (½ package)

Heat oven to 350° F.

In large skillet, brown meat and onion lightly. Spread in shallow 10-by-10- or 9-by-13-inch baking dish. Spread vegetables over meat, making an even layer. Stir together soup and milk until smooth. Drizzle soup mixture over vegetables. Arrange Tater Tots in single layer over soup.

Bake 1 hour or until Tater Tots are browned.

Not everyone appreciated Pop Art. When Andy Warhol's first Campbell's Soup Can paintings went on display in a Los Angeles art gallery in 1961—for $100 apiece—another gallery down the street defiantly stacked soup cans in it windows with the sign: "The real thing, 29¢."—from the book, *60s!* by John and Gordon Javna (New York: St. Martin's Press, 1988)

Biscuit-Topped Beef and Vegetable Casserole

Let's sing lustily: "Our state fair is a great state fair." On my annual pilgrimage to the Minnesota State Fairgrounds in St. Paul, I never miss the Horticulture Building. It is a great place to admire the wonderful range of fresh vegetables grown in the Midwest. There you can admire the displays of carrots, green beans, sweet corn, many types of potatoes, squash in many colors and shapes, peppers, kohlrabi, and radishes. Their glowing natural colors promise the best of nutrition and flavor. This is a great way to use fresh carrots and celery.

MAKES 4 TO 6 SERVINGS

⅛ cup chopped onion

2 tablespoons olive or vegetable oil

1 pound regular or lean ground beef

1 teaspoon salt

⅛ teaspoon pepper

1½ cups tomato juice, divided

2 cups chopped celery (3 ribs)

2 cups diced carrots (3 medium)

3 drops Tabasco hot pepper sauce

⅓ cup catsup

¼ cup all-purpose flour

1 can refrigerated biscuits (10 biscuits)

Stir-fry onion in oil in large skillet (I use my 12-inch electric fry pan). Crumble beef and add to skillet. Brown beef while adding salt and pepper. When meat is browned, drain off excess fat. Add 1 cup of the tomato juice, celery, carrots, and Tabasco. Simmer covered for 15 minutes.

Heat oven to 375° F.

In small bowl, whisk together remaining ¼ cup tomato juice, catsup, and flour, forming a thick sauce. Stir tomato sauce into meat-vegetable mixture. Cook, stirring constantly until thickened. Pour mixture into 2-quart casserole. Top hot mixture with biscuits.

Bake 20 to 25 minutes, until biscuits are done and casserole is bubbling.

Cooks' Notes

Whenever using biscuit dough, refrigerated or homemade, in a hot dish, the filling has to be hot at the time the biscuits are added. If not, the bottoms of the biscuits do not cook quickly enough, and the tops will be brown and the bottoms gooey.

 Variation

Speedy Beef and Vegetable Casserole: Use 4 cups frozen mixed vegetables instead of carrots and celery.

Menu Idea!

BACK TO THE FIFTIES

Biscuit-Topped Beef and Vegetable Casserole

Lettuce Wedge with Thousand Island Dressing

New-Fashioned Fruit Crisp (recipe page 156)

Meat 'n' Potatoes Hot Dish

Folks from two neighboring states sent two versions of this filling dish. The pork version (with milk added to soup) came from Judy Tyler Eklund of Afton, Iowa, my friend since college. Her husband Dale raises pigs; officially he's a pork producer. She often helps him "sort" the hogs, which means choosing which animals are ready to be sold. On a long-ago visit, Judy was needed in the pig barn just at the time her houseguests (my daughter and myself) were ready for breakfast. No problem. Judy put pitchers of orange juice and milk on the table and the coffee cake and scrambled eggs in the oven. We helped ourselves and soon Judy shed her barn boots and sat down for a cup of coffee.

Arva Zabel gave me the beef version, which is made with cream-style corn instead of the milk. Arva reared seven children on dairy farms near Barron, Wisconsin. Son Rick has fond memories of coming home after school to find that Mom had baked bread and, better yet, had churned butter. He and his siblings dearly loved the fresh butter on the homemade bread. This casserole went into the oven right after the bread.

MAKES 4 TO 6 SERVINGS

1 pound bulk pork sausage, ground pork, or regular or lean ground beef

1 or 2 slices onion, chopped

10-ounce can cream of mushroom soup

¾ cup milk or 15-ounce can cream-style corn

3 to 6 cups peeled and sliced raw potatoes

Nature's Seasoning or a favorite seasoning mixture

¾ cup grated cheese, Cheddar or processed cheese (optional)

Heat oven to 350° F.

Brown pork with onion in a large skillet, using a wooden spoon to break up chunks. Drain excess fat—there won't be much. Whisk soup and milk or corn together. Using a 2- to 3-quart baking dish, layer half the potatoes, sprinkling with a little seasoning. Add a layer of meat and half the soup mixture. Repeat with layers of potato, meat, and soup. Transfer casserole to oven.

Bake about 1 hour, until potatoes are tender and top of mixture is browned. Sprinkle with cheese; return to oven until cheese melts.

 **Variation**

Meat, Potatoes, and Mushroom Hot Dish: Stir 4-ounce can drained mushrooms stems and pieces into soup before layering ingredients.

 Cooks' Notes

Jump-start baking by covering casserole and microwaving it 5 to 6 minutes on high, then placing in preheated oven. Mixture should test done in 30 to 35 minutes.

A menu idea for this hot dish is on page 161.

The Cedric Adams Hot Dish

When I came to live in Minnesota in the mid-1950s, Cedric Adams was a well-known radio personality. He read the news on WCCO Radio and everyone knew his distinctive voice. It was said that in summer you could walk down the street at 6 p.m. and from every home you could hear the voice of Adams reading the news. Later, he worked on WCCO-TV, and the late Betsy Breckenridge Norum often prepared the recipes that were featured on his noontime program. Betsy was a member of the Kamera Kitchen staff at Betty Crocker Kitchens at General Mills. The producer gave her the script for the program, and she prepared two batches—one to use as a stand-in for setting up the lights and the second to be shown on camera. Time was tight and she often took a cab from the General Mills headquarters in Golden Valley to the studio downtown. Those of us working in the Kitchens were always eager to hear about the excitement of broadcasting live from the studio. And Adams loved good food. Besides this casserole, he had a sandwich named for him—a combination of bread, sliced turkey, and a rich cheese sauce.

MAKES 4 TO 6 SERVINGS

1 medium onion, chopped (1 cup)
2 tablespoons butter, margarine, or olive or vegetable oil
1 pound lean ground beef
¾ teaspoon salt
⅛ teaspoon ground black pepper
6 cups coarsely shredded cabbage (packaged coleslaw also works well), divided
10½-ounce condensed tomato soup, stirred to liquify

Heat oven to 350° F.

Grease 2-quart baking dish or spray with vegetable oil spray. In large skillet, stir-fry onion in butter. Add ground beef, salt, and pepper, heating meat through and breaking it up with spoon, but not browning it. Spread 3 cups cabbage in bottom of baking dish. Cover with meat mixture. Top with remaining cabbage. Over the whole business, pour the can of tomato soup.

Cover and bake 50 to 60 minutes or until cabbage is tender. When using freshly shredded cabbage, take off the cover after 30 minutes of baking or the dish will be soupy.

 **Variations**

Tightwad Hot Dish: Use only ½ pound ground beef.

Cedric Talks Turkey: Use 1 pound ground turkey in place of beef.

 Menu Idea!

SIXTIES-STYLE SUPPER

Cedric Adams Hot Dish

Baked Potatoes

Cornbread or Corn Muffins with Honey

Watermelon Pickles or other Sweet Pickles

Hidden Fruit (Canned Fruit under Vanilla Pudding)

Corned Beef Casserole

This is one of the many recipes in this collection that uses a canned cream soup. Years ago when the soups were first manufactured, they quickly replaced homemade white (or cream) sauce. Cooks were happy to open a can rather than having to cook a sauce. Cream soups are often requested at the neighborhood food shelf where I volunteer. The cream soups, including cream of potato, are a valued and versatile item for low-income cooks. These soups along with vegetables, fruits, peanut butter, and tuna, come from nearby supermarkets or from scout troops, churches, and all sorts of charitable drives. They can be cooked to serve as a lunch or light supper, or they can be combined with tuna and a vegetable and served over toast or noodles as a main dish. Our shelf serves primarily the working poor, including new immigrants from Russia, Mexico, Somalia, and Sudan.

MAKES 6 SERVINGS

10½-ounce can cream of mushroom, celery, chicken or chicken mushroom soup

1 cup milk

1 cup finely cubed American, Cheddar, Monterey Jack, or colby cheese (4 ounces)

1 cup uncooked elbow macaroni or small shell macaroni

¼ cup finely chopped onion

12-ounce can corned beef, diced

¾ cup buttered crumbs (optional)*

*Toss ¾ cup dry bread crumbs with 2 tablespoons melted butter

Heat oven to 350° F.

Stir soup and milk together to make sauce. Add the cheese, macaroni, onion, and diced corned beef; mix well. Pour into greased 1½-quart casserole dish.

Top with crumbs, if using them. Bake 1 hour or until macaroni is tender.

Overnight option: After pouring corned beef mixture into casserole, cover and refrigerate 3 to 4 hours or overnight. An hour before the meal, top with crumbs and bake as directed.

 Variations

Dried-Beef Casserole: In place of corned beef, use dried beef from 2½-ounce jar, cut in strips, and two sliced hard-cooked eggs.

Easy Shaved-Beef Casserole: In place of corned beef, use shaved roast beef from the meat counter, cut in strips.

Menu Idea!

DINNER DOWN ON THE FARM

Corned Beef Casserole or
Meat 'n' Potatoes Hot Dish (recipe page 62)

Sliced Garden Tomatoes

Salad of Leaf Lettuce and Green Onions

Yeast Buns with Favorite Preserves

Fresh Strawberries or Raspberries with Cream

Pizza Rice

Joe Blade, a confirmed bachelor who worked at the *Star Tribune* newspaper in Minneapolis, lived on steaks and chops for some years. Then he discovered cookbooks by writers such as Julia Child and Joseph Pasternak and began to enjoy working in the kitchen. After spending Saturday afternoon creating a beautiful platter of Chicken Paprikash, for example, he was perfectly happy to eat the dish every night after work. He prepares this toothsome combination in the microwave, but I like to set it and forget it, so I adapted it for the oven. It keeps well and loses nothing in the reheating.

MAKES 4 TO 6 SERVINGS

3 cups cooked long-grain rice

1 cup prepared pizza sauce

¾ cup water

½ pound Italian sausage, removed from casing and crumbled

3 to 6 cups sliced fresh mushrooms

1 medium bell pepper, cored and diced, or ¾ cup frozen chopped pepper, thawed

heaping ¼ cup green pimento-stuffed olives, halved

2 ounces pepperoni sausage slices, cut up (½ cup)

½ cup grated Parmesan cheese

1 cup shredded mozzarella cheese

Heat oven to 350° F.

Using a 3-quart casserole, stir together the rice, pizza sauce, water, crumbled sausage, sliced mushrooms, chopped pepper, olives, and pepperoni. Cover casserole with a lid or a sheet of aluminum foil.

Bake 30 to 35 minutes, stirring once or twice, until mixture is piping hot. Remove from oven and stir in the cheeses. Again, cover the casserole and set aside until cheeses melt. Stir before serving.

Norte-Americano Tamale Pie

Mention tamales and I recall buying the special corn husks to prepare tamales at home in the mid-1970s. It required a drive to the far side of the Twin Cities, to Morgan's Mexican Lebanese Foods on South Robert in West St. Paul. This full-to-the-brim store was run by a hard worker named Morgan, whose Lebanese wife with her family produced some of the area's first pita (pocket) breads. Located in the thriving area that serves immigrants from Mexico, their business name linked the two countries.

Tamales are delicious little bundles of cornmeal dough filled with a savory meat-tomato-corn mixture. The fingers of the Mexican cooks fly as they assemble them, then put them on to steam. For a big batch, everyone pitches in to shape the dough around the filling, then wrap it all in a corn husk for cooking. It's the sort of happy gather-round-and-chat cookery that every culture seems to have. This simple pie brings twenty-first-century ease, via canned vegetables and packaged muffin mix, but keeps the authentic flavor.

MAKES 6 SERVINGS

¾ pound ground turkey or regular or lean ground beef

½ pound ground pork

⅓ cup chopped onion

1 large clove garlic, minced

14-ounce can petite diced tomatoes or 10-ounce can tomatoes with green chilies

15-ounce can whole kernel corn, drained, or 2 cups frozen corn

1½ to 2 teaspoons chili powder

¾ teaspoon salt

¼ teaspoon cayenne pepper

TOPPING

8½-ounce package corn muffin mix

1 egg

⅓ cup milk

Heat oven to 350° F.

Cook and stir turkey or beef and pork in wide skillet. Add onion, garlic, tomatoes, corn, chili powder to your taste, salt, and cayenne pepper. Continue cooking 10 minutes, stirring frequently. Turn mixture into 9-inch round or square casserole.

In medium bowl, stir together corn muffin mix, egg, and milk. Spread corn muffin batter over meat mixture in casserole. Bake until mixture is bubbling and topping is set, about 30 minutes.

Drink sweet milk after eating onions to eliminate onion breath. Drink black coffee after eating garlic to eliminate garlic breath. —from *The Four Seasons of Homemaking,* edited and compiled by the homemaking staff of radio station WWJC-Duluth (1965)

Cabbage and Sausage Supper

In recent years, the members of the crucifer family of vegetables have been highly touted as a source of antioxidants and other health-promoting nutrients. But among all the crucifers, cauliflower, Brussels sprouts, and cabbage seem to take a back seat these days to broccoli. Broccoli's lovely green "trees" are wonderful, adding color and flavor to many a plate. But versatile, long-keeping, always-inexpensive cabbage deserves to be rediscovered. Buying shredded cabbage, labeled coleslaw mix, shortens up the preparation time considerably for this filling hot dish.

MAKES 6 SERVINGS

2 cups Thick Cream Sauce (recipe page 168)

2 tablespoons prepared mustard, yellow ballpark or Dijon-style

14- or 16-ounce ring smoked sausage

7½ to 8 cups shredded cabbage or 16-ounce package coleslaw mix

1 cup grated Cheddar cheese

2 tablespoons fine bread crumbs, such as Progresso brand

Prepare white sauce. Stir mustard into sauce, blending well.

Heat oven to 350° F.

Remove casing from sausage and cut it into bite-size chunks. Grease 10-inch square baking dish or other 2-quart casserole. Arrange half the cabbage in bottom of dish. Top with half the sausage chunks, then pour on half the mustard sauce. Complete with second layers of cabbage, sausage, and sauce. Top with cheese, distributing evenly, then do the same with the crumbs.

Bake covered 35 to 40 minutes, until bubbly. If using freshly shredded cabbage, remove cover after 20 minutes of baking. Refrigerate leftover casserole to reheat for lunch the next day.

 **Variation**

Cabbage and Frank Supper: Use cut-up wieners in place of sausage.

 Cooks' Notes

There will be some liquid in the bottom of the dish after serving—cabbage is very high in water—but during refrigeration leftover casserole will absorb liquid.

A FRANK BY ANY OTHER NAME

We Americans love our franks, our wieners and hot dogs, our kielbasa, too. Origins differ—frankfurters hail from Frankfurt, Germany; wieners from Vienna, Austria; kielbasa from Poland. But these smoked precooked sausages with their sprightly seasonings go so well with so many foods. A wiener served in a soft roll is the beloved midgame treat at baseball games; in fact, the yellow mustard slathered in hot dogs is sometimes labeled "ballpark" mustard. Franks work well in hot dishes—no browning needed—just cut 'em up.

Ham-Broccoli Bake

When you serve this delicious hot dish to your family or friends you are providing them with one of the five-to-nine daily servings of fruits and vegetables recommended for Americans. As a longtime member of Minnesota's 5-a-Day for Better Health Coalition (recently renamed "Fruit and Veggies—More Matters"), I know that people in Minnesota typically eat 3 to 3½ servings of fruits and vegetables daily. No, French fries don't count. Getting these vital nutrients isn't as hard as it sounds. Enjoy a glass of juice with breakfast, vegetable soup at lunch, a piece of fruit as an afternoon snack, and a serving of vegetable plus a salad at dinnertime. One portion equals ½ cup of canned or cooked fruit or vegetable, 1 cup of juice, ¼ cup dried fruit such as raisins, 1 cup leafy greens or a whole piece of fruit, such as an apple or orange. I suggest serving this casserole with a side dish of baked winter squash and, for dessert, baked apples. That's energy smart as well as nutrition smart.

MAKES 5 SERVINGS

2½ cups cut-up fresh broccoli or frozen broccoli cuts

1½ cups cubed cooked or baked ham or turkey ham

1 cup drained canned or frozen whole onions

2 cups Medium Cream sauce (recipe page 168)

2 teaspoons dry mustard or 3 teaspoons prepared mustard

½ cup grated Cheddar cheese

1 cup buttermilk baking mix, such as Bisquick

½ teaspoon celery seed

⅓ cup milk

Heat oven to 425° F.

Mix broccoli, ham, and onions in 1½-quart baking dish. Prepare white sauce, adding mustard and cheese and stirring until smooth. Pour sauce over ham mixture.

Place in oven while making biscuits. In small bowl, stir together biscuit mix, celery seed, and milk, forming a soft dough. Remove baking dish from oven and drop 10 small biscuits atop ham mixture, holding a tablespoon in one hand and rubber spatula in your other hand to shape each biscuit.

Bake 15 to 20 minutes, or until ham and vegetables are bubbling and biscuits are golden brown.

 **Variations**

Turkey-Broccoli Bake: Use smoked turkey from the deli in place of ham.

Ham-Vegetable Bake: Use 3½ cups frozen California mix (cauliflower, broccoli, and carrots) in place of broccoli and onions.

Swiss Ham–Broccoli Bake: Try Swiss cheese in place of Cheddar in sauce.

Chicken with Rice and Two Soups

This is one recipe to turn to when you need to put a main dish in the oven while you're away for two hours. In some families, it's hockey or swimming practice that prompts this choice. If that's the case, the young athletes will appreciate having an entrée ready when they arrive home starved. In my case, I like to have a main dish baking in the oven while I attend church. Setting the oven to turn off automatically is most helpful, in case services run late. I'm especially fond of the rice that soaks up the other flavors.

MAKES 4 TO 6 SERVINGS

1 cup uncooked white rice or 1¼ cups brown rice or wild rice (or mixture of the three)

2½- to 3-pound broiler-fryer chicken, cut up, or 1¼ pounds boned chicken breasts or thighs

1 envelope dry onion soup mix

10¾-ounce can cream of mushroom soup

2½ cups water, as needed

Heat oven to 325° F (300° F for glass pan).

Spread rice in bottom of 9-by-13-inch baking pan. Arrange chicken pieces on rice, skin side up. If using chicken breasts, cut breasts into halves with kitchen shears. Pour onion soup mix into small bowl and stir together the enclosed bouillon granules and the dried onion. Sprinkle onion mixture evenly over chicken pieces. In medium bowl, stir soup and 2 soup cans (2 ½ cups) of water together; pour over all. Cover pan with sheet of aluminum foil.

Bake 2 hours.

HOUSE BRANDS AND THE SMART SHOPPER

A generation ago, the soups used in this favorite dish were brand name products. The mushroom soup was Campbell's, the dry onion soup, Lipton's. No more. Now house brands are offered by every food chain. Due to the advertising and promotion budgets for the name brands, the difference in price between the two may be substantial. But there may be a difference in quality, too. The only way to find out is to buy both and do a side-by-side comparison.

Salmon Supreme

As we Americans have become more and more concerned about obesity and fats in the diet, salmon has entered the spotlight as a delicious source of health-promoting omega-3 fatty acids. Once we depended on wild sources of this fish. Now, due to the science of aquaculture, farm-raised salmon and other fresh-water fish are readily available at a reasonable cost. When I visit my cousins in Seattle, we feast on planked fresh salmon, but here in the landlocked Midwest, we usually serve the canned variety.

MAKES 6 SERVINGS

15-ounce can pink salmon

10¾-ounce can cream of chicken, mushroom, or celery soup

½ cup sour cream

¼ cup minced onion

⅛ teaspoon black or white pepper

3 cups cooked white or brown rice (1 cup uncooked)

9-ounce package frozen cut asparagus or 2 cups diced fresh asparagus

1 cup grated Cheddar, Monterey Jack, or Swiss cheese

Heat oven to 350° F.

Drain salmon, reserving liquid; break salmon into chunks. (Remove any skin, but do not remove bone, as it is digestible and a good source of calcium.) Combine soup, salmon liquid, sour cream, onion, and pepper in saucepan. Heat briefly, then stir in rice. Gently fold in salmon. Turn into greased, shallow 2-quart baking dish. If using frozen asparagus, place in a sieve and rinse under cold tap water to remove ice crystals. Scatter asparagus over rice-salmon mixture. Sprinkle with cheese.

Bake 20 to 25 minutes or until bubbling.

 **Variations**

Tuna Supreme: Use 9-ounce can tuna, drained, in place of salmon.

Crab Supreme: Use 1½ cups imitation crab in place of salmon.

Salmon Supreme with Peas or Green Beans: Use 1½ to 2 cups frozen green peas or frozen cut green beans in place of asparagus.

Menu Idea!

FRIDAY NIGHT FISH BAKE

Salmon Supreme

Easy-Bake Carrots (recipe page 112)

Spinach Salad with Sliced Fresh Mushrooms

Garlic Toast

Lemon Sherbet

*(pour on a little crème de menthe for grown-ups,
a dollop of chocolate syrup for children)*

Green and Gold Casserole

Wherever women gather, the talk often turns to cooking and the swapping of favorite recipes. We swap menu plans and food ideas on the bus on the way home in the evening, at coffee breaks in the office, and after the business is done at church and club meetings. Years ago, I was part of a group of women who collected and repaired used clothing to be sent to Africa. My daughter Barbara, a toddler at the time, went along and played in the nursery at the Quaker church in Minneapolis where the group met. As we turned jeans with torn knees into shorts and sewed on missing buttons, we talked over plans for supper or recipes for the next potluck. I was soon scribbling amounts and directions and asking about casserole sizes and baking times. A saint by the name of Barbara Parrott shared this combination of spinach and cheese, which I immediately loved and later featured in the Taste section of the *Star Tribune*. A novelty at the time, vegetarian entrees like this are now frequently served. Food can be nutritious and flavorful—without meat.

MAKES 6 SERVINGS.

1½ cups cottage cheese

½ pound American process cheese, such as Velveeta, cut up (2 cups)

10-ounce package chopped frozen spinach, thawed and drained

4 eggs, beaten

4 tablespoons flour

Heat oven to 350° F.

Combine cottage cheese, American cheese, drained spinach, beaten eggs, and flour. Pour into a greased 1½-quart baking dish.

Bake until set and top is brown, 70 to 75 minutes.

Variation

Use 9-ounce package frozen asparagus cuts or broccoli cuts in place of spinach.

Menu Idea!

MAKE MINE MEATLESS

Carrot, Celery, and Red Pepper Sticks
with Seasoned Yogurt Dip

Green and Gold Casserole

Big Bowl of Caesar Salad

Hot, Crusty Whole Grain Rolls with Honey Butter

Peach Cobbler (recipe page 154)

Hot Dishes for Potlucks and Church Suppers

Beef Chow Mein Hot Dish

Heavenly Hash

Seafood Lasagna

Enchilada Fiesta

Reuben Bake

Cowboy Beans

Pork Chop Bake

Polish Quarterback Casserole

Turkey Tetrazzini

Golden Glow Casserole

Casserole of Shrimp and Deviled Eggs

MY INTRODUCTION to the potluck supper came as a youngster living in small-town Iowa. Every so often, our church held a potluck supper in its basement. We would all ride together to church. Mom held the hot dish in her lap. It was wrapped first in a section or two of newspaper, then in a big white dish towel, with the opposite corners tied together for a practical carry-along handle.

When the table was laden and everyone was assembled, we sang grace and lined up, ready to fill our plates. I have a strong memory of my mother bending down to whisper to my brother and me, "Let the pastor and his family go first." That was fine—the pastor's children were schoolmates. No one was surprised to see that the one pan of fried chicken, brought by a farm family, held little but a wing after the first family had filed by. No matter, I liked scalloped corn and baked beans just as much as chicken.

Nowadays, potluck means "anything goes." It matters not whether the food is homemade or store-bought, it's breaking bread together that counts—sharing a meal, a bit of news, a laugh or two.

Beef Chow Mein Hot Dish

This was *the* after-funeral casserole at my church, Lutheran Church of the Good Shepherd in Minneapolis, for many years. Typically, ten of us, members of the Christian Service Circle, gathered in the church kitchen the morning of the service. First, the hot dish went into the oven, then we would turn to mixing salad, buttering bread, and cutting bars. We enjoyed working together and were happy to be able to help the grieving families in this practical way. Nowadays we serve thick sandwiches, a fresh vegetable tray (with dip), a big fruit salad, and an array of bars. We believe that folks facing several hours' drive home deserve a good meal. After the lunch, family and friends often linger, sharing stories about the deceased.

MAKES 10 SERVINGS

1½ pounds regular or lean ground beef

1 to 2 large onions, diced (1½ to 3 cups)

16-ounce package frozen mixed vegetables (corn, peas, and green beans)

1 cup chopped celery

½ to ¾ cup cashews (optional)

2 (10¾-ounce) cans chicken with rice soup

4-ounce can mushrooms

2½ cups Medium Cream Sauce (recipe page 168) or 2 (10¾-ounce) cans cream of mushroom soup

8-ounce package chow mein noodles*

*Taste noodles before using—if they taste stale, discard and buy fresh.

Heat oven to 350° F.

Brown ground beef and diced onions in large skillet (we used cast iron) until meat loses its red color. Add the mixed vegetables, celery, cashews, rice soup, mushrooms, white sauce, and most of the noodles. Mix well and spread in a 9-by-12-inch baking dish. Top with rest of noodles.

Bake 50 to 60 minutes, until bubbling.

Cooks' Notes

Serve immediately. If held in oven, noodles will get gluey.

 ## Variation

Beef Oriental Casserole: Use 16-ounce frozen Oriental-style mixed vegetables (often containing water chestnuts) in place of the corn-pea-bean mixture.

Menu Idea!

COMFORT IN A BUFFET MEAL

Beef Chow Mein Hot Dish

Apple Cole Slaw with Sweet-Sour Dressing (toss diced apple and shredded cabbage with sweet-sour dressing)

Buttered French or Vienna Bread

Help-Yourself Raw Vegetables with Creamy Dip

Platters of Bars—such as Brownies, Pumpkin, and Lemon

Heavenly Hash

This satisfying casserole includes protein (beef and cheese), carbohydrates (noodles and corn), and a goodly amount of vegetables. All you need with it is a wedge of lettuce with a favorite salad dressing. If your schedule permits, take the hash out of the oven and cover to keep it warm. Then turn up the oven to 375° F to bake refrigerated crescent rolls—golden in just twelve minutes.

MAKES 8 TO 10 SERVINGS

2 tablespoons butter

1 medium onion or ¾ cup chopped frozen onion, thawed

1 rib celery, sliced

1 green pepper, diced

8 ounces fresh mushrooms (about 2 cups whole mushrooms), sliced, or 4-ounce can mushrooms, drained

1½ pounds regular or lean ground beef

8 ounces egg noodles (half a 1-pound bag)

8-ounce package cream cheese or Neufchâtel cheese

15-ounce can whole kernel corn, drained, or 2 cups frozen whole kernel corn

10¾-ounce can tomato soup

Heat oven to 350° F.

Melt butter in large skillet. Stir-fry onion, celery, pepper, and mushrooms in butter; add meat and stir-fry, breaking up meat, about 10 minutes. Meanwhile, cook noodles according to package directions in lightly salted water, being careful to cook them just to the al dente stage— "to the tooth" or offering some resistance when bitten into. Cut cream cheese into 15 to 18 chunks and turn into a large mixing bowl. Drain excess fat from skillet of meat and vegetables. Add meat and vegetables to cream cheese in bowl. Toss with two large spoons until hot ingredients are coated with cream cheese. Drain noodles and add to bowl, again tossing to combine. Next add drained corn; toss again. Finally, pour on soup, continuing to toss lightly. Turn hash mixture into 2-quart baking dish.

Bake 40 to 45 minutes, until well heated.

COLLECTING COOKBOOKS—A CONSUMING HOBBY

My kitchen and nooks all over the house display my cookbook collection. Some 350 volumes, down 150 since I decided to share books I no longer use with the food classes at the College of St. Catherine, St. Paul. I still own my first cookbook, the two-volume *Meta Given's Modern Encyclopedia of Cooking* (1951). (A half-century later I marvel at the use of the word *modern!*) Some books were brought back from trips, others were gifts. One entire shelf holds books by the constantly evolving Betty Crocker of General Mills—I worked on eleven of them. During my years on the Taste section, new cookbooks poured in from publishers hoping for reviews. The spring freshet of books was three to five per week; the fall deluge, seven to eight books weekly. The best were reviewed or included in a feature article. Occasionally, I browsed at a used bookstore with a trove of older cookbooks (the owner bought entire libraries from prominent citizens). My library has been invaluable in researching this book.

Seafood Lasagna

Who says this beloved layered casserole has to be made with tomato sauce? It's equally delicious made with a creamy sauce and studded with seafood or beef. The beef version at the end is popular in South Dakota, according to food writer Mary Gunderson, who grew up in Irene. That's no surprise when you know how important beef production is in South Dakota. In fact, beef is produced—and served often—in all five of the states featured in this book.

MAKES 8 SERVINGS

10 lasagna noodles (½ pound)

2½ cups Medium Cream Sauce (recipe page 168)

⅓ cup sliced green onions

1 teaspoon minced garlic

1 teaspoon crushed dried basil

12 ounces frozen uncooked shrimp

7-ounce can crab meat

2 cups creamed cottage cheese or ricotta cheese

¾ cup grated Parmesan cheese

⅓ cup plus 2 tablespoons minced parsley, divided

3 cups shredded mozzarella cheese

Cook lasagna noodles as directed on package. Drain well and keep separated by laying flat between pieces of waxed paper. Prepare Medium Cream Sauce. Stir green onions, garlic, and basil into sauce. Set out shrimp—it will thaw as you work; drain crab meat. Stir together cottage cheese, Parmesan cheese, and ⅓ cup parsley.

Heat oven to 350° F.

To assemble lasagna, spread small amount of cream sauce in 9-by-13-inch baking dish. Make layers as follows: 4 lasagna noodles (overlap slightly to cover bottom of pan), ½ of cottage cheese mixture, ⅓ of the sauce, ½ of seafood (alternate shrimp and chunks of crab meat), and ⅓ of mozzarella cheese; 3 noodles, remaining cottage cheese, ⅓ of sauce, ½ of seafood, and 1/3 of mozzarella cheese; last 3 noodles, and remaining mozzarella cheese.

Bake 40 minutes or until hot and bubbly. Let stand about 10 minutes, then sprinkle with remaining parsley. Cut into squares.

 **Variation**

White Lasagna with Beef: Follow directions for Seafood Lasagna making these substitutions: Replace shrimp and crab meat with 1½ pounds regular or lean ground beef that has been cooked—but not browned—with 1 cup chopped onion, 2 to 4 cloves garlic (minced), ½ teaspoon salt, and ⅛ teaspoon white pepper. Do not add green onions, garlic, and basil to Cream Sauce; instead season sauce with nutmeg to taste. Stir beef mixture into Cream Sauce.

Layer as follows: 4 noodles, ½ of cottage cheese mixture, ½ of beef-cream sauce, and ⅓ of mozzarella cheese; 3 noodles, remaining cottage cheese, remaining beef-cream sauce, and ⅓ of mozzarella; last 3 noodles and remaining mozzarella. Bake as directed.

Enchilada Fiesta

From the Southwest via South Dakota comes this satisfying combo. I spotted in it *From South Dakota with Love* by sister-authors Debra and Laurie Gluesing. This hot dish has all the flavor of a typical enchilada without the work of filling and rolling the tortillas.

I keep corn tortillas on hand most of the time to use in a Mexican toasted cheese sandwich I like a lot. Simply put a slice of cheese and a slice of luncheon meat—such as honey ham—between two corn tortillas. Then cook in a cast iron skillet (no oil necessary) over medium heat until cheese melts, sealing the sandwich. Watch closely so it doesn't burn.

MAKES 8 SERVINGS

1½ pounds regular or lean ground beef

¾ cup chopped onion

1½ teaspoons cumin seeds (optional)

1 teasoon salt

Pinch of garlic salt or garlic powder

1¼ teaspoons chili powder

¼ cup water

12 (5½-inch) corn tortillas

15-ounce jar mild taco sauce

12 ounces sour cream (¾ of 16-ounce carton)

4 cups shredded Colby-Jack cheese (part Cheddar may be used)

Heat oven to 375° F.

Brown ground beef and onion; drain. Combine with cumin, salt, garlic salt, chili powder, and water. Simmer 10 minutes. Place 6 tortillas on bottom and up sides of greased 13-by-9-inch pan, overlapping as necessary. Spread ¾ cup taco sauce over tortillas; spread meat mixture over taco sauce. Top with sour cream. Sprinkle with half of cheese. Put 6 tortillas over cheese, again overlapping. Top tortillas with remaining taco sauce and sprinkle with the rest of the cheese. Cover pan with aluminum foil.

Bake 35 to 40 minutes, until bubbling. Uncover and bake 5 minutes longer.

Menu Idea!

MEXICALI MENU

Guacamole with Tostada Chips

Enchilada Fiesta

Stir-Fried Zucchini Slices with Red Pepper Strips

Mango Chunks (fresh or canned) with Heavy Cream

Reuben Bake

For some twenty years, I've been fascinated as I've watched the Reuben flavor combination be adapted to other foods. First came the thick grilled sandwich: rye bread generously filled with slices of corned beef, turkey, and Swiss cheese, and a big wad of sauerkraut, all slathered with Thousand Island Dressing. Presumably it was named for its creator, the operator of a Jewish delicatessen. Next came the Rachel sandwich, identical to the Reuben, but with fresh cole slaw in place of the kraut, assembled, not grilled. Later came Reuben Salad, the same ingredients tossed with greens—and plenty of Thousand Island, of course. And for wintertime, there's Reuben Soup. It's a thick, chowder-style, cream-based soup with the requisite meats, cheese, and kraut; rye croutons can top it or toasted deli rye slices accompany it. Here's the hot dish version.

MAKES 4 TO 6 SERVINGS

About 2 pounds fresh or canned sauerkraut

4 slices bacon, chopped

3 tablespoons apple juice or water

1 onion, chopped (about 1 cup)

1 apple, peeled and diced

½ teaspoon caraway seed

2 medium ripe tomatoes, sliced, or equivalent drained diced canned tomatoes

2 to 3 tablespoons Russian or Thousand Island dressing

8 large slices cold cooked corned beef (about ½ pound)

1½ cups shredded Swiss cheese

Heat oven to 400° F.

Wash the kraut, drain it, and squeeze it dry. In a 10-inch skillet, fry the bacon until crisp. Add the drained kraut and continue to stir-fry until kraut is lightly brown. Add the apple juice, onion, apple, and caraway seed. Cover and allow to steam briefly over low heat while you assemble the rest of the ingredients. Spread the kraut mixture over the bottom of an 8-by-12- or 9-by-9-inch baking dish. Top with tomatoes. Spread the dressing over the tomatoes. Cover tomatoes with corned beef slices, then sprinkle evenly with cheese.

Bake 10 to 20 minutes, until hot throughout.

Menu Idea!

SUPPER? ACH, JA

Reuben Bake

Green Beans

Leaf Lettuce with favorite Creamy Dressing

Deli Rye Bread

Blackberry Cobbler (recipe page 154.)

Cowboy Beans

You may know this hearty dish as Calico Beans or Five-Bean Hot Dish. Whatever you call it, folks love it, and it stays warm a good long time on the buffet or potluck table. It's one of those versatile dishes that is good whatever combination of beans you find in the cupboard. Use either bacon or beef, if you'd rather. Or skip the meat entirely; it's your call. Leftovers are excellent the second day—add some catsup or barbecue or tomato sauce as you reheat the beans.

MAKES 8 TO 10 SERVINGS

¼ pound bacon

½ pound regular or lean ground beef

1 cup chopped onion (1 medium)

15-ounce can baked beans

3 (14- or 15-ounce) cans assorted beans— kidney, pinto, garbanzo (chickpeas), lima or butter, your choice

⅔ cup catsup

½ cup brown sugar

¼ cup vinegar

Heat oven to 325° F.

Fry bacon in 9- or 10-inch skillet; drain, cool slightly, then crumble. Place beef in skillet, stirring to break it up and brown it. Add onion to beef and stir-fry until transparent. Turn beef mixture into 3-quart casserole or bean pot. Add baked beans. Open, rinse, and drain the three cans assorted beans; stir into mixture in casserole. Stir catsup, brown sugar, and vinegar into bean mixture. At this point you can add your own touch: a dollop of mustard, some chopped apple, or some barbecue sauce.

Bake covered 1½ hours or until bubbly.

 ## Variations

Not-Exactly New England Baked Beans: Use two 28-ounce cans baked beans instead of the combination of different canned beans; omit ground beef and double the bacon. Use only ¼ cup brown sugar and add ¼ cup real maple syrup.

Spirited Baked Beans: Prepare Cowboy Beans (above) using ½ cup bourbon in place of the ¼ cup vinegar.

 ## Cooks' Notes

Cowboy Beans can be doubled or tripled when you're serving a crowd. Think Boy Scout or softball banquet. Mix the ingredients and bake it in big oblong pans. A flat pan may dry out more quickly, so check during baking in case you need to add more liquid.

Menu Idea!

COME AND GET IT

Cowboy Beans

Corn Bread or Corn Muffins

Cole Slaw with Pineapple Tidbits

Chocolate Cake with Fudge Frosting

Pork Chop Bake

All five midwestern states—North and South Dakota, Iowa, Minnesota, and Wisconsin—produce hogs, the source of the chops and bacon, popular ingredients for hot dishes. Pork has been raised here since the pioneers carried piglets and led sows as they traveled to their new homes. And in their knapsacks was salt pork (salt-preserved pork fat), a staple, along with corn meal and coffee. Old-time farms raised grain crops, chickens, dairy cows, vegetables, apples, and pigs, aiming to feed themselves and, with luck, have something to sell. But, as more land was cleared, farmers began to specialize. One might concentrate on livestock and buy the feed grain from another. Now, Iowa is the top pork state, and Des Moines, Iowa, is home to the National Pork Producers. On their Web site, *www.theotherwhitemeat.org,* the Pork Producers offer pork cookery expertise to the nation. In adapting this 1970s recipe for today's kitchen, I had to switch from thin chops to thicker ones that would match the cooking time of the rice. Today's pork has been bred to be much leaner than the meat of the past. And thin-cut lean meat cooks very quickly, more quickly than the rice.

MAKES 4 SERVINGS

Three 1¼-inch thick boneless pork chops

Flour for coating

2 tablespoons olive or vegetable oil

1 cup uncooked white rice

2 large tomatoes

1 large onion

½ green pepper, halved crosswise (for rings)

½ teaspoon salt

¼ teaspoon leaf thyme or oregano

⅛ teaspoon freshly ground pepper

1½ cups chicken or beef broth

Heat oven to 350° F.

Cut each chop in half. Dredge pork pieces in flour and brown in hot oil in large skillet, about 5 to 8 minutes. Grease a 9-inch-square baking dish. Spread rice in prepared dish and arrange pork pieces on top. Slice tomatoes and cut onion and green pepper into rings. Distribute vegetables over chops. Sprinkle on seasonings and then pour broth over ingredients.

Cover and bake 1 hour or until rice is tender and pork is done.

Menu Idea!

PORK IN THE SPOTLIGHT

Pork Chop Bake

Corn Pudding (recipe page 30)

Sliced Cucumbers with Sour Cream

Mint Ice Cream

Favorite Chocolate Cookies

Polish Quarterback Casserole

Lots of chefs write cookbooks, but few ordinary guys do. Of course, Mike Triggs is no ordinary guy. He loves life, cooking, and entertaining. A little book he wrote called *Picnics on a Whim* sums up his joie de vivre. We met when a tipster recommended him for a *Star Tribune* Taste feature story. We bonded over our mutual love of cooking and the fact that he came from Charles City, Iowa, where I lived briefly as a toddler when Dad managed the weekly paper there. Mike, a one-time political party organizer, turned Mall of America haberdashery sales-man, created this hot dish for the get-togethers he loves to host. It's got every-thing: meat, veggies, cheese, and great flavor.

MAKES 6 SERVINGS

5 to 6 russet baking potatoes

½ pound Polish sausage (3 links)

¼ cup milk

2 tablespoons butter or margarine

½ cup grated Swiss cheese

½ cup grated Cheddar cheese

½ 10-ounce package frozen chopped spinach
or 1 cup cooked, chopped spinach (optional)

½ cup crushed potato chips (optional)

Heat oven to 350° F.

Boil potatoes in skins in 1 inch boiling, salted water until tender, 20 to 30 minutes. Meanwhile, remove casing from sausage and cut into bite-size pieces. Pour water off potatoes. Holding potatoes with a two-tine kitchen fork, remove skins. Place potatoes in large mixing bowl and mash. Add milk, butter, and cheeses; beat until smooth. If using frozen chopped spinach, place it in a sieve and run under tap water to remove ice glaze; drain and squeeze well. Stir chopped spinach into potatoes. Fold sausage into potato mixture. Spoon into 2⅓-quart buttered casserole dish. Top with crushed potato chips if using. Bake 30 to 40 minutes or until golden brown.

 **Variation**

Italian Quarterback Casserole: Use mild Italian sausage in place of Polish sausage.

Menu Idea!

FROM IOWAY

Polish Quarterback Casserole

Coleslaw with Carrots and Olives

Watermelon Pickles

Buttermilk Biscuits

Chocolate Chip Cake (add ¾ cup
miniature chocolate chips to batter for
white cake mix before baking as directed)

Turkey Tetrazzini

Betty Crocker Kitchens in Golden Valley was my work home in the late 1950s and early 1960s. I learned a great deal about recipe development and about teamwork. In 1958, Betty, our icon, was being transformed from a baking expert to an authority on entertaining. To that end, General Mills contracted with a New York writer, Llewellyn Miller, for a book called *Easy Entertaining*. The cosmopolitan Miss Miller came to Minnesota to confer with those of us working on the recipes for her book. This delectable casserole was featured in the Midnight Suppers chapter. It rated raves from the homemakers on the "Minneapolis 30" home testers panel. They liked having the choice of alternate ingredients. I've served this tetrazzini regularly since then, most recently for a quiet holiday dinner.

MAKES 6 SERVINGS

6 ounces uncooked spaghetti

2 cups cooked turkey, cut in small pieces

½ cup cubed cooked ham or ¼ cup crumbled cooked bacon

¼ cup chopped green pepper or 4-ounce can pimento, chopped

1 cup pitted ripe olives, cut into large pieces, or ½ pound fresh button mushrooms, halved

1 egg yolk, beaten

¼ cup butter

6 tablespoons flour

1 teaspoon salt

¼ teaspoon ground white pepper

2 cups chicken or turkey broth

1 cup half-and-half

3 tablespoons dry sherry (optional)

½ cup grated Parmesan cheese or slivered almonds

Heat oven to 350° F.

Heat water to a rapid boil in a large kettle. Break spaghetti in 2-inch pieces. Cook according to package directions. Drain, rinsing with hot water.

While spaghetti is boiling, combine turkey, and ham or bacon, pepper or pimento, and olives or mushrooms in a mixing bowl. Separate the egg yolk from white and have yolk ready to add. Melt butter over low heat in heavy saucepan. Blend in flour and seasonings. Cook and stir, with heat on low, until the flour paste is smooth and bubbly. Remove pan from burner, stir in half the broth. Return to heat and cook, stirring frequently, while gradually adding remainder of broth and the half-and-half. Boil sauce 1 minute—this eliminates any floury taste from uncooked flour. Remove from heat and stir in sherry, if using. Turn the drained spaghetti into the sauce and toss with two large spoons until pasta is coated with sauce. Stir egg yolk into hot pasta mixture. Then add the pasta to turkey mixture in bowl, again tossing to distribute ingredients.

Pour into a 2-quart baking dish—I use a big square shallow Corelle dish. Sprinkle on cheese or almonds. Bake 25 to 30 minutes.

Golden Glow Casserole

The combination of cheese, mayonnaise, and tomato sauce makes a golden sauce, which sets off the crab and shrimp in this hot dish beautifully.

MAKES 4 TO 6 SERVINGS

1 cup grated sharp Cheddar cheese

6½-ounce can crabmeat or 1 cup cut-up imitation crab

5-ounce can shrimp or 6-ounce can tuna or salmon, drained

3 cups cooked medium shell macaroni

½ cup mayonnaise or salad dressing

8-ounce can tomato sauce (1 cup)

½ cup chopped green onion

Heat oven to 350° F.

In mixing bowl, combine cheese, crabmeat, shrimp, or tuna or salmon, shell macaroni, mayonnaise, tomato sauce, and green onion. Spray or butter a 2-quart baking dish. Turn casserole mixture into baking dish.

Bake about 25 minutes, or until browned and bubbly.

"PUT A FEATHER IN YOUR CAP AND CALL IT MACARONI."

The original versions of the recipes in this collection were made with elbow macaroni or with broken noodles simply because that was the pasta widely available in the 1950s. But the pasta horizon has widened. Now cooks can choose from many interesting shapes. It's fun, too, to learn the Italian names for these shapes. Look for *radiatore* (radiator), *penne* (pen point), *rotini* (twist), *cappelletti* (little hat), *orecchiette* (little ear), and so on. You can vary your favorite hot dishes by not only switching the meat or fish, but also by using a different pasta. If you're really into pasta, check the refrigerated section at the market for fresh pasta—particularly tortellini—or, if you live in a city, look for an Italian market that sells freshly made pastas along with authentic meats, cheeses, and sweets.

Casserole of Shrimp and Deviled Eggs

Adapted from *Favorites Old and New*, published in 1965 by Lutheran Church Women of St. Paul's Lutheran Church (formerly Icelandic Lutheran) of Minneota, Minnesota, hometown of my favorite poet and essayist, Bill Holm.

MAKES 6 SERVINGS

3 cups cooked white or brown rice

6 hard-cooked eggs

2 tablespoons mayonnaise

¼ teaspoon dry mustard

¼ teaspoon salt

Dash of pepper

3 tablespoons butter

4 tablespoons flour

½ teaspoon salt

3 cups milk

¼ cup diced American or grated Cheddar cheese

1½ cups canned shrimp

1 cup soft bread crumbs (1 slice)

2 tablespoons melted butter

Heat oven to 350° F.

Spread rice in greased 2½-quart casserole. Make the deviled eggs: Peel and cut eggs in half; scoop out yolk and mash with mayonnaise, mustard, salt, and pepper. Spoon filling back into the egg whites. Arrange atop rice. Make white sauce of butter, flour, salt, and milk in pan over medium heat. Add grated cheese and cook until melted. Remove membrane (it's the digestive tract) from shrimp. Arrange shrimp around deviled eggs. Pour sauce over eggs and shrimp. Toss crumbs and butter; top casserole with buttered crumbs.

Bake 25 to 35 minutes.

 Cooks' Notes

To use frozen raw, shelled, deveined shrimp: Measure shrimp into kitchen sieve. Rinse under tap water to remove ice glaze. Arrange as directed. Bake just until shrimp turns pink and sauce is bubbly, about 25 minutes.

 Menu Idea!

FISH FOR FRIDAY—OR ANY DAY

Casserole of Shrimp and Deviled Eggs

Easy-Bake Carrots or Asparagus (recipe page 112)

Lettuce and Spinach Tossed with Mushrooms and Bacon

Banana Slices Layered with Strawberry Sauce and Vanilla Yogurt

5

Satisfying Side Dishes

Bacon 'n' Tomato Beans

Spinach Soufflé

Broccoli-Rice Magnifique

Easy-Bake Carrots

Everyone-Loves-This Corn Casserole

M . . . m . . . m Good Potatoes

Squash Gourmet

Pecan-Topped Sweet Potato Casserole

Always-Great Zucchini Hot Dish

Spoon Bread a la Lady Bird

Whole Grain Pilaf

Crunchy Wild Rice Casserole

"EAT YOUR CARROTS—they will help you see in the dark." "Eat those bread crusts—they will make your hair curly." "Eat your spinach, it will make you strong like Popeye the Sailor Man." Parents of the past used such admonitions to nudge their children toward eating vegetables and other foods high in nutrients, not to mention foods that might go to waste. (Fruits—naturally sweet and well liked—weren't subject to such urgings.) Cooks did what they could to enhance good-for-you vegetables and whole grains. A selection of their successful approaches—adding cheese or nuts, mushrooms, sour cream, or eggs—appear here. These side dishes can share the oven with a roast or meat loaf or casserole—thus saving energy. While dinner is in the oven, you can make a dessert from my dessert chapter or a cake from a mix. Then everyone will see how super-organized you are.

Bacon 'n' Tomato Beans

The green bean casserole made with mushroom soup and topped with onion rings is widely used, but it's not the only way to present the popular beans. Anyone who is fond of bacon and tomato sandwiches, or a bacon and tomato salad, will enjoy this dish.

MAKES 4 SERVINGS

4 strips bacon

14½-ounce can stewed tomatoes with green pepper and onions

3 tablespoons real mayonnaise

2 cups frozen cut green beans (from 16-ounce bag)

1 teaspoon Worcestershire sauce

1 cup bread crumbs tossed with 2 tablespoons melted butter

Heat oven to 350° F.

In 2-quart saucepan, fry bacon until crisp. Drain on paper toweling. Pour off all except 2 tablespoons bacon fat. Add tomatoes to saucepan and simmer 5 minutes or so to reduce liquid. Add mayonnaise, stirring until well distributed. Stir in beans, Worcestershire sauce, and crumbled bacon. Pour into 8-inch round baking dish. Top vegetables with crumbs.

Bake 15 to 25 minutes, until hot throughout and crumbs are brown.

 Variations

Fresh Green Beans with Bacon 'n' Tomato: Use 8 ounces (2 cups) cut fresh beans; precook in pan or in microwave, 10 minutes.

Garlicky Bean Casserole: Use garlic-herb croutons in place of buttered crumbs.

Spinach Soufflé

Making a soufflé requires a kitchen technique called "folding." You need a rubber spatula and a supple wrist. Spread the light mixture—whipped egg whites—on top of the heavier mixture—the spinach-cheese mixture here. With the pan in one hand and the spatula in the other, cut into the middle of both layers, across the bottom of the pan and up the nearest side. Turn the pan a quarter-turn and repeat the down, across, and up motion. Repeat until the whites are evenly distributed into the spinach mixture. Don't overdo it—you'll release the air trapped in the whites before it reaches the oven where it should expand, pouffing the soufflé.

MAKES 4 TO 6 SERVINGS

10¾-ounce can cream of chicken soup

1 cup shredded sharp Cheddar cheese

⅛ teaspoon nutmeg

4 eggs, separated

9-ounce package frozen chopped spinach

¼ teaspoon cream of tartar

Heat oven to 400° F.

In medium saucepan, heat and stir soup, cheese, and nutmeg until cheese melts. Beat egg yolks until thick and slowly add to soup and cheese mixture. Cook spinach as directed on package. Drain spinach and stir into soup mixture. Beat egg whites with cream of tartar until stiff. Fold whipped egg whites into soup mixture. Pour into 2-quart casserole.

Bake for 30 minutes, until puffed and golden. Serve immediately.

Broccoli-Rice Magnifique

This hot dish dates to the 1970s when many a recipe had a Frenchified name. Since then we've moved to Italian-style names—things became Delicioso or Primo. By the time the nineties rolled around it was Tex-Mex that intrigued us and we were adding terms like Pico and Grande. This combination usually goes into my oven on the spur of the moment. It's very versatile, having been served with everything from pan-broiled burgers to roast pork tenderloin. And even with a substitution or two, it's still great. The chicken variation below is from *Schmeck's Gut!*, published in 1988 by Sisters of the Century in celebration of the centennial of the city of Ashley, North Dakota.

MAKES 6 SERVINGS

½ to 1 cup fresh or frozen chopped onion

1 cup chopped celery

3 tablespoons butter or vegetable oil

16-ounce bag frozen broccoli cuts, thawed*

2 cups cooked white, brown, or wild rice

1¼ cups bottled cheese dip, such as Cheez Whiz

10½-ounce can cream of mushroom, celery, or chicken soup, undiluted

*No time to thaw broccoli? Just rinse it under cold tap water to remove ice glaze.

Heat oven to 350° F.

Stir-fry onion and celery in butter or oil in large skillet. Stir in broccoli, rice, cheese product, and soup. Turn into 2-quart casserole.

Bake 35 to 45 minutes, or until hot throughout.

 **Variations**

Broccoli-Chicken Magnifique: Add 2 to 3 cups chopped cooked chicken.

Spinach-Rice Magnifique: Use two (9-ounce) packages chopped spinach in place of broccoli.

Broccoli Gourmet: Use sliced water chestnuts or jicama instead of celery.

North Dakota history professor Tom Isern penned a 2003 essay, "Plains Folk: Hot Dishes" in which he delves into the origins of these dishes. He wrote:

"What I have come to question, though, is the idea that the hot dish (a.k.a. casserole) is a particularly Lutheran (or Norwegian or Swedish or German) institution. I investigated this in the collections of the Institute for Regional Studies at North Dakota State University. What I discovered by browsing the TX (food) shelves is that well into the twentieth century, hot dishes were almost unknown in Lutheran circles.

Where hot dishes first showed up was in the cookbooks of Anglo-American women in such institutions as the Federated Women's Clubs. The convenient casserole resulted from the drive for efficiency and timesaving in the kitchens of women with English surnames. Lutherans and other descendants of more recent immigrants adopted hot-dish ways later."

Easy-Bake Carrots

As a brand-new homeowner in 1960, I decided to turn a corner of the backyard into a vegetable plot. I remembered the sweet carrots in my mother's Victory garden in the little town of Strawberry Point, Iowa. My husband happily spaded the ground and I knelt beside the hoed row to press in the tiny carrot seeds. We watered. We waited. In due time, the stalks poked through; then came the feathery green leaves. Yes! When I couldn't wait any longer, I pulled one. The little carrot was round and chunky for about two inches, exactly the depth of the fill dirt that was spread over the clay soil before the house was built. Beyond two inches, the carrot shriveled to nothing; the root had found little nourishment in the dense clay. From then on, I planted veggies that grew above ground: zucchini, tomatoes, cucumbers, and spinach. Fortunately, I could buy carrots and other root vegetables at the bountiful produce counter at a Lunds store two blocks away. This preparation is from the late Ken Kelley, a former colleague at Betty Crocker Kitchens.

MAKES 4 SERVINGS

10 ounces shredded carrots, packaged or freshly shredded

1 tablespoon sugar

1 teaspoon salt

Cracked pepper as desired

3 tablespoons butter, melted

Heat oven to 350° F.

Place carrots in medium bowl. Add sugar, salt, and pepper; toss well. Pour on butter and toss again to coat carrots with butter. Turn into 1-quart baking dish.

Cover and bake 50 minutes to 1 hour, or until tender.

 **Variations**

Asparagus Bake: Use 1 pound fresh asparagus. Wash, break off tough ends and cut into 2-inch pieces. Omit sugar. Use 2 tablespoons olive oil in place of butter. Bake at 375° about 10 minutes or until you smell the distinctive aroma.

Parsnip Bake: Prepare 3 cups shredded parsnips: peel parsnips to remove protective waxy coating (it's edible, but not great), then shred parsnips, using hand shredder or shredding disc on food processor. Bake as directed for carrots.

Everyone-Loves-This Corn Casserole

Here is a Thanksgiving standard from Lucia Hickman, an avid reader and good neighbor.

MAKES 4 TO 6 SERVINGS

1¼ cups crushed saltine crackers (27)

1 cup milk

2 eggs, beaten

3 tablespoons melted butter

2 tablespoons minced onion

½ teaspoon Worcestershire sauce

1 cup milk

6.5-ounce can minced clams

1 cup whole kernel corn, frozen or canned, drained

¼ teaspoon salt

½ cup shredded Cheddar cheese (optional)

Combine crackers, milk, beaten eggs, and butter in small bowl and let stand about 30 minutes. Add minced onion, Worcestershire sauce, milk, clams (with liquid), corn, and salt; mix well. Turn into 1½-quart casserole.

Bake (no need to cover) at 325° F for 35 to 40 minutes. Sprinkle cheese over mixture and return to oven for another 5 to 10 minutes, until knife inserted in center comes out clean.

 **Variations**

Corn Casserole with Oysters: Use ¾ cup fresh or canned oysters in place of clams.

Quick Corn Casserole: Omit clams, but use 2 cups whole kernel corn.

Fresh Corn Casserole: Prepare dish with fresh-cut corn: simply cook ears of fresh corn (1 to 2 ears depending on size) in boiling water about 3 minutes (to set the milk); cool ears and use sharp knife to cut kernels cutting about 3 rows at a time until ear is stripped.

M...m...m Good Potatoes

Marian Gunderson's children and grandchildren always ask for these potatoes for family celebrations. Marian, who lives in Yankton, South Dakota, serves in the state legislature and is a longtime community volunteer. Marian's daughter Mary, a former Taste colleague, shared her mother's recipe.

MAKES ABOUT 6 SERVINGS

6 medium potatoes, boiled in skins and cooled (2 pounds)

¾ to 1 cup sour cream

¾ to 1 cup milk

¼ cup fresh or dried chopped chives

1 to 2 teaspoons paprika

½ teaspoon salt

⅛ teaspoon white pepper

Heat oven to 350° F.

Remove skins from boiled, cooled potatoes. Grate potatoes into 2-quart casserole dish (I use the grating disc on the food processor). Fold in sour cream and milk, starting with ¾ cup each. Mealy potatoes such as russets will absorb more liquid than waxy potatoes such as whites or reds. The potato mixture should be soft but not sloppy. Season with chives, paprika, salt, and pepper. Sprinkle top with more paprika.

Bake about 1 hour or until bubbly and golden.

 **Variation**

Do-Ahead Potatoes: Make Good Potatoes up to 24 hours ahead. Refrigerate. If chilled, bake 10 minutes longer.

Menu Idea!

HAPPY BIRTHDAY TO YOU

Broiled Steak

M . . . m . . . m Good Potatoes

Big Tossed Salad

Garlic Bread

Lemon Pudding

Squash Gourmet

Adapted from *Ken Kelley Cooks* (1977, Abbott Hospital Auxiliary). And hereby hangs a tale. Kenena (Ken) MacKenzie Kelley served as speech writer for the Betty Crocker Kitchens' director and booklet editor at General Mills for 20-plus years. Barely five feet tall, she swirled into our office, swathed in a flowing cape. Canadian-born, she had a trace of an accent and a cackle of a laugh. She loved to cook and entertain. The potluck supper at her porch-wrapped home on Lake Minnetonka was a highlight of each summer for the Betty Crocker staff. Enthralled by the house, I once asked her how she could bear to leave it, especially when the breeze was up across the lake. She looked me right in the eye and said, "If I didn't leave it, we wouldn't have it." Ever candid, she explained that husband Bill, who worked with "adult male criminals" (as a probation officer), did not pull down the sort of wages needed to support a lakeside home. In retirement, Ken taught cooking classes to groups of younger women, who dubbed themselves the Copy Cats. After her death, the women collected her recipes in a book bearing her name. They quoted her creed: "Cooking will never be dull or boring if you try a new idea, a new seasoning or a new recipe at least once a week."

MAKES 4 SERVINGS

Hubbard squash large enough to provide 2 cups cubed squash
¼ cup sliced green onions, including some green tops
1 cup sour cream
2 to 3 tablespoons cream or milk
Salt and pepper to taste

Heat oven to 350° F.

Cut squash in half; remove seeds and pith. Bake squash cut side down in shallow pan 45 to 60 minutes, or until fork tender, but not soft; baking time depends on size of squash. Remove squash skin and cut into 1-inch cubes; refrigerate or freeze remaining squash for another use. Transfer squash cubes to a 1-quart casserole. Sprinkle with sliced onions. Thin sour cream with cream or milk. Pour cream mixture over squash; toss to distribute evenly. Sprinkle squash with salt and pepper; toss again.

Bake 20 to 25 minutes, until steaming hot.

Pecan-Topped Sweet Potato Casserole

From my friend, Virginia Clausen Behrens, wife, mother, and grandmother, gardener, cook, and friend, all rolled into one smiling package. As girls in Strawberry Point, Iowa (population 1,000), we walked to grade school together; then, in the classroom, vied for the teacher's attention, waving our hands to answer her questions. Though her husband Doug was a dairy farmer, he also raised a few pigs for fall butchering. On my daughter Barb's first visit to the farm at the age of three, she was thrilled at the sight of the baby pigs heading for their feeder. "Little pigs, little pigs," she cried. But the hungry piglets, pushing and shoving, clanging the self-feeder lids, did not jibe with the adorable pictures of the three little pigs in her storybook. Ducking her head, she ran for the safety of Virginia's back stoop and the quiet of her kitchen.

MAKES 8 TO 10 SERVINGS

40-ounce can sweet potatoes or 5 cups cooked and peeled sweet potatoes (about 4 pounds before cooking)

½ cup granulated sugar

2 eggs

⅓ cup butter, at room temperature

⅓ cup milk

1 teaspoon vanilla

TOPPING

¾ cup brown sugar

1 cup chopped pecans

⅓ cup flour

⅓ cup butter, melted

Heat oven to 350° F.

Drain potatoes. Mash potatoes with the granulated sugar, eggs, butter, milk, and vanilla. Turn into a buttered 2-quart baking dish. Prepare topping: Combine brown sugar, pecans, flour, and melted butter. Distribute topping evenly over sweet potato mixture.

Bake 35 to 40 minutes, or until knife inserted in center comes out clean.

 **Variation**

Coconut-and-Pecan-Topped Sweets: Add 1 cup flaked or shredded coconut to the topping mixture.

 Menu Idea!

IOWA-STYLE COMPANY DINNER

Baked Ham or Roast Chicken

Pecan-Topped Sweet Potato Casserole

Microwaved Asparagus Spears or Whole Green Beans

Favorite Fruit Gelatin Salad

Brown 'n' Serve Rolls

Cookies or Cupcakes from the Freezer

Always-Great Zucchini Hot Dish

Once upon a time I wanted to grow my own zucchini—after all, I knew from the grapevine that anybody could grow zucchini. The first year, all went well. The plants had big floppy green leaves, then beautiful elongated fruit, which I prized and cooked. The second year, I planted the seedlings and stood back to admire the leaves and wait for the fruit. To my dismay, almost overnight the luxuriant leaves wilted, and the plants turned a sickly yellow. I sought the advice of a kind but taciturn neighbor. "Borers," he announced. Sure enough, we dug up the plants and there they were, those ugly borers. Too late, I learned that the borers burrow down into the soil in the fall and stay there. Come spring, they crawl back up to the top, ready to devour what the unwitting gardener has provided for them. Since then, I've gotten my zucchini at the farmers market. Whether you grow 'em or buy 'em, this is a wonderful way to eat 'em. Use bagged shredded carrots from the produce department to speed preparation. I began making this dish after it was touted by Peggy Katalinich of Greendale, Wisconsin, formerly editor of the Taste section, now food director of *Family Circle* magazine.

MAKES 6 SERVINGS

6 cups sliced unpeeled medium zucchini (4 to 5)

1½ cups shredded carrots (2 to 3)

½ cup chopped onion

3 tablespoons butter, melted, or olive oil, divided

10¾-ounce cream of chicken soup

1 cup sour cream

1 to 1½ cups seasoned croutons

Heat oven to 350° F.

Precook zucchini until tender-crisp—the microwave is fastest. Stir-fry carrots and onion in 2 tablespoons of the butter or olive oil until onion is tender. Combine soup and sour cream. Fold in drained vegetables and half the croutons. Pour into greased 2-quart casserole. Stir together remaining croutons and last tablespoon of butter. Sprinkle croutons over casserole. Bake 20 to 25 minutes, until heated all the way through.

 **Variation**

Zucchini-Chicken Hot Dish: Stir 1 to 1½ cups diced, cooked leftover chicken into vegetable mixture.

Menu Idea!

WEEKEND PATIO PARTY

Grilled Rib Eye Steaks

Corn on the Cob

Always-Great Zucchini Hot Dish

Platter of Sliced Tomatoes and Cucumbers

Strawberries or Raspberries
Topped with Ice Cream

Spoon Bread a la Lady Bird

Meal made from dried corn has nourished midwesterners for 150 years, ever since the first settlers moved into the area covered by the Louisiana Purchase. The years from 1850 to 1900 were especially challenging for cooks, wrote Marjorie Kreidberg in *Food on the Frontier*. She quotes a letter from a woman named Susan Adams, written in 1856 just after her family had arrived at their shanty near Shakopee, Minnesota: "I made a fire and we soon had a meal of pork and cornmeal mush which we ate with thankful hearts."

When I was growing up during World War II, we had corn bread often. We liked to split the square of hot corn bread making two surfaces to spread with butter and honey. And if there was some corn bread left, we'd ask mother to heat it in the oven and we'd pour on pancake syrup as a dessert of sorts after our morning bowl of oatmeal.

Later, when I had the pleasure of traveling in Europe, I learned about polenta. Using plain cornmeal, Italians cook it with water or milk, then spread it in a shallow pan and chill it, before lifting out pieces to fry and serve as a crusty side dish. Polenta is tasty with additions such as stir-fried mushrooms or diced red pepper. Polenta is so popular now that it is being sold precooked, packed in a tube, refrigerated, and ready for frying. But spoon bread gets my vote.

Southern cooks made this casserole of cornmeal mush, mixed with milk, eggs, and butter, famous. Beloved all over the country, it is a favorite accompaniment to ham, pork roast, and fried chicken. This recipe is purported to be from Claudia Taylor "Lady Bird" Johnson, wife of the late president, Lyndon B. Johnson.

MAKES 4 TO 6 SERVINGS

1 cup cornmeal

3 cups milk, divided

3 eggs, well beaten

3 teaspoons baking powder

1 teaspoon sugar

1 teaspoon salt

2 tablespoons butter

Heat oven to 350° F.

Using a medium saucepan, stir cornmeal into 2 cups of the milk. Bring to a boil making cornmeal mush. Fold in remaining milk and the beaten eggs. Stir in the baking powder, sugar, salt, and butter. Turn into a 1½-quart baking dish.

Bake 30 to 40 minutes or until top is set and flecked with golden brown. Serve with melted butter or gravy. To reheat, cut in squares and heat in the microwave oven; top with maple syrup or pancake syrup.

Whole Grain Pilaf

I use whole grains often, not only because I like their crunchy texture and nutty flavor, but also because of their top-rated nutrient density. Nutrient density refers to how many nutrients (vitamins, minerals, fiber, protein, or carbohydrates) a food furnishes proportionate to the calories. Dr. Julie Jones of the College of St. Catherine, St. Paul, has become a national spokesperson for the importance of whole grains in the diet. Citing an ever-mounting body of research, she explains that whole grains have many components that act locally in the digestive tract. They work systemically to improve gut health, reduce risk of coronary disease, type 2 diabetes, stroke, and hypertension. They may also be helpful in improving immune response.

Julie chaired an international conference on whole grains in 2005, bringing together cereal scientists from around the globe. To demonstrate the versatility and range of whole grains, she worked with chef Paul Lynch to plan meals for the conferees. For seven days, the kitchen at the downtown Minneapolis Radisson Hotel featured grains, from bulgur to wild rice, in every single meal.

MAKES 6 SERVINGS

2 tablespoons butter, margarine, or vegetable oil

½ cup chopped green or white onions

½ pound fresh mushrooms, sliced (shiitake recommended)

1 cup bulgur wheat or medium barley

Water*, chicken broth, or beef bouillon, 2 cups for wheat or 2½ cups for barley

½ cup slivered almonds (optional)

* if using water, add ½ teaspoon salt with the grain

Heat oven to 350° F.

Stir-fry onions and mushrooms in butter or oil until brown. Stir in wheat or barley and brown lightly, 1 to 2 minutes. Add water, broth, or bouillon and bring to a boil, stirring constantly. Pour into 1½-quart casserole.

Cover and bake until liquid is absorbed and grains are tender: wheat pilaf for 20 to 25 minutes, barley pilaf for 30 to 35 minutes. If using almonds, add to dish about 15 minutes before end of baking time.

 ## Variations

Rice Pilaf: Use wild or brown rice in place of wheat or barley; bake 45 to 60 minutes.

Mixed-Grain Pilaf: Use ⅓ cup each prepared wild rice, medium barley, and brown rice; add 1 clove garlic, minced, with onion.

 Menu Idea!

DINNER'S READY WHEN YOU ARE

Roast Turkey Breast or Pork Tenderloin

Easy Whole Grain Pilaf

Shredded Carrot Salad with Toasted Sesame Seeds

New-Fashioned Fruit Crisp (recipe page 156)

Crunchy Wild Rice Casserole

This recipe, from Susan Henderson of St. Paul, Minnesota, surely dates to the "old" days when wild rice was very expensive and therefore often extended with white rice. At the time, much of the country's supply of wild rice came from northern Minnesota and Canadian lakes, harvested by hand and roasted by Indians. Then someone hit on the idea of producing the wild grass in paddies just like white rice. Farmers in Minnesota and California latched on to this idea and began cultivating paddies and building the machinery needed to facilitate the growing and harvesting. Soon, wild rice, prized for its nutty flavor and great texture, was widely available and much lower in price. So popular is wild rice that you can now buy it fully cooked in a can or frozen, mixed with white rice. The availability of wild rice has prompted creative cooks to add it to many types of foods, yeast breads being the most interesting of them.

MAKES 6 TO 8 SERVINGS

½ cup wild rice

1½ cups water

10-ounce can chicken consommé

½ cup long grain white rice or brown rice

3 tablespoons butter

1 cup chopped onion

1 cup sliced fresh mushrooms

1 cup chopped celery

5-ounce can sliced water chestnuts, drained

¼ cup soy sauce

½ cup toasted slivered almonds

Place wild rice in large saucepan with water. Boil 5 minutes, then remove from heat and let stand 1 hour. Drain off excess water. Set aside.

Pour consommé into the saucepan. Bring to a boil and add precooked, drained wild rice. Simmer 20 minutes. Add white rice and return to boil. Simmer 15 minutes covered. Start heating oven to 350° F. In a large skillet, melt butter and stir-fry onions, mushrooms, celery, and water chestnuts. Place rice mixture, vegetable mixture, soy sauce, and almonds in 3-quart casserole. Mix well using two large spoons.

Bake 30 to 45 minutes, until hot and fragrant.

 ## Variation

All-Wild Rice Casserole: Use 1 cup wild rice, omit white rice.

 ## Cooks' Notes

Cooked wild rice (plain) will keep six months in the freezer. Uncooked wild rice will keep up to ten years in an airtight container.

FOUR EASY WAYS TO COOK WILD RICE

1 cup uncooked wild rice = 3 to 4 cups cooked wild rice
1 pound wild rice measures about 2¾ cups uncooked wild rice

On the Range Top: Bring 4 cups water or chicken broth to boiling in a heavy saucepan; stir in 1 cup wild rice. Simmer, covered, about 45 minutes or until tender but not mushy—grains will open up and curl. Remove cover; fluff rice with fork. Simmer 3 minutes longer. Drain if necessary.

In the Conventional Oven: Stir 1 cup wild rice into 4 cups hot water or chicken broth in a 1½-quart casserole with lid. Bake, covered, at 350° F. 1 hour. Check rice and, if needed, add more water. Fluff with fork and continue baking another 20 minutes. Cooked rice should be moist.

In the Microwave Oven: Stir 1 cup wild rice into 4 cups hot water or chicken broth in a 4-quart baking dish (a large glass bowl can be used). Cover and microwave on High 30 to 35 minutes, stirring every 10 minutes. Cook until rice is tender and grains have opened; let rice stand, covered, 15 minutes.

The Soaking Method: Mix rice into 3 cups boiling water in saucepan. Bring to boil and boil 5 minutes only. Remove from heat; let stand, covered, 1 hour or longer; drain. Complete cooking by boiling in salted water to cover 30 minutes, or until tender.

"Keep an ear peeled for argument—especially if your guests don't know each other very well. If you're all old friends and you know that Fred and Larry have fought the battle of the last election every week for a year, ignore it. But if you've brought people together for the first time and voices begin to rise over politics, religion or any other controversial subject, create a distraction. Turn on the phonograph and invite one of the combatants to dance with you. Solicit advice on what you should do about the zinnia bed or the curtains in the children's room. Do anything that will separate the antagonists, conversationally and physically."

From "A Handbook for the Hostess: Presenting the Party," in *Betty Crocker's Hostess Cookbook* copyright © 1967 by General Mills, Inc. (New York: Golden Press).

 Menu Idea!

THE HUNTER'S HOME FROM THE HILL

Mugs of Hot Tomato Juice

Roast Venison, Duck, Pheasant, or Rabbit

Crunchy Wild Rice Casserole

Carrots and Green Peas

Crescent Rolls

Fruit-ful Cobbler (recipe page 154)

Breakfast and Brunch Casseroles

ARE YOU A LARK or an owl? We larks are the early risers, those who greet the morning with a song. The owls are, of course, the night owls, those who get through the day just fine, but really come alive about 9:00 o'clock in the evening and go right on until 2:00 AM. We larks love breakfast, at home and away. Owls may sip some coffee or brisk tea, but prefer to wait awhile before breaking their fast. Brunch, served any time from 9:00 AM on through 1:00 PM, works for both types. The morning hot dishes in this chapter will make fine additions to your repertoire of quiches, pancakes, waffles, and made-to-order omelets.

Do-Ahead Brunch Casserole

Studying nutrition at Iowa State University in the '50s, I learned that eggs are a source of highly digestible protein and therefore desirable as a food for infants, the infirm, and the elderly. They are also a great value—excellent protein at a nominal price. And for singles like myself, one egg can be the centerpiece of a simple meal. Fifties food expert Peg Bracken commented wryly on the popularity of the egg with solo cooks, saying that some of her friends ate so many eggs, they cackled! I have long enjoyed an egg in the morning—scrambled, baked, microwaved—bring it on. This casserole takes kindly to embellishments. During my research, I found versions with twice the sausage—or different cheeses—or added vegetables. Folks love them all. This recipe is from *Marvelous Minnesota: Cookbook of the Minnesota Federation of Women's Clubs* (1953). P.S. Brunch ought to end with dessert.

MAKES 6 TO 8 SERVINGS

1 pound pork sausage

2 to 2½ cups herbed croutons

2 cups shredded sharp Cheddar, mozzarella or Monterey Jack cheese

4 eggs

¾ teaspoon dry mustard

2 cups milk, divided

1 can cream of mushroom soup

Brown sausage, breaking into chunks; drain well. Place the croutons in a greased 9-by-13-inch pan or baking dish. Top croutons with the cheese, making an even layer. Next, distribute browned sausage over the cheese. Beat together eggs, mustard, and 1½ cups milk. Pour egg mixture over layered ingredients. Cover pan; refrigerate overnight.

In the morning, heat oven to 300° F. Whisk together the soup and ½ cup milk; pour into dish. Bake, uncovered, 1 to 1½ hours, or until puffed and brown.

 **Variations**

Sausage-Lovers' Brunch: Use two pounds favorite breakfast sausage.

Mushroom-Lovers' Brunch: Stir-fry 8 ounces sliced fresh mushrooms in butter and add to mushroom soup mixture.

Vegetarians' Brunch: Omit sausage and mushroom soup layer. Cover croutons with 1 cup finely chopped zucchini, 1 cup chopped red pepper, 1 cup diced tomato; sprinkle cheese over vegetables.

Menu Idea!

COME FOR BRUNCH

Grapefruit and Orange Compote
with Pomegranate Seeds

Do-Ahead Brunch Casserole

French-Style Green Beans Almondine

Date-Chocolate Chip Cake with Ice Cream

Hash Brown Quiche

If you came to my Park Row Bed & Breakfast in St. Peter, MN, during its eight years of business, you would certainly have had this casserole, the Sunday special. My daughter Barb had spotted the recipe in an article in *Midwest Living* magazine and suggested I test it as I made plans for starting a B&B. She likes the egg-and-cheese quiche filling and much prefers potatoes to pastry. It's rich, colorful, and infinitely adaptable. Best of all, it is equally delicious as a supper dish offered with a green salad and a light, lemony dessert. The combination of pepper Jack cheese and Swiss is inspired—the nutty Swiss balancing the "heat" of the pepper-spiked cheese.

MAKES 6 SERVINGS

3 cups frozen hash-brown potatoes, thawed enough to measure, or refrigerated loose-pack hash browns

¼ teaspoon seasoned salt or no-salt seasoning blend, such as Mrs. Dash

1 cup diced cooked ham, such as Hormel Cure 81 (6 ounces)

1 cup shredded pepper Jack cheese (4 ounces)

1 cup shredded Swiss cheese (4 ounces)

¾ cup half-and-half or fat-free half-and-half

3 eggs or equivalent low-cholesterol egg substitute, such as Eggbeaters

Heat oven to 425° F.

Spray a 10-inch pie plate with vegetable oil spray. Press hash browns onto bottom and up sides of pie plate forming a crust. Sprinkle lightly with seasoned salt or seasoning blend.

Bake 20 to 25 minutes, until potato edges start to brown. Remove from oven.

Lower heat to 350° F. Toss together ham and cheeses; spread in crust. Beat half-and-half and eggs. Pour over ingredients in crust.

Bake uncovered for 25 to 30 minutes or until knife inserted in center comes out clean. Let stand 10 minutes before serving.

 ## Variation

Canadian Quiche: Use Canadian bacon in place of ham and Cheddar cheese in place of pepper Jack cheese.

SUPERMARKETS SERVE CONVENIENCE

Busy cooks can find more and more ingredients ready to use right from the supermarket. For this recipe, for example, you can buy the ham already diced and the Swiss cheese already shredded. When you spot a new convenience form of a favorite ingredient, buy a small quantity and compare it to the old ingredient. Then decide whether the convenience is worth the money spent and time saved. A case in point is frozen cooked noodles. I skip them. I always have noodles on hand and can easily keep an eye on a pan of boiling noodles, cooking for 7 or 8 minutes, as I dovetail it with arranging a relish tray or tearing up lettuce for salad.

Cheese-Rich Oven Omelet

A generous Mankato, Minnesota, cook by the name of Bev Smith shared this recipe with me in the early days of my St. Peter bed-and-breakfast. It is her Christmas morning entrée, she said, which explains the red pimento and the green parsley highlighting the rich cheese. It soon became popular with my guests. I passed it along to the readers of *Wake Up and Smell the Coffee*—Lake States Edition, a collection of bed-and-breakfast recipes compiled by Laura Zahn. If a member of the family or a guest is a vegetarian, add the bacon last, taking out one portion just before that addition and baking the all-cheese omelet in an individual ramekin.

MAKES 6 SERVINGS

½ cup fried, crumbled bacon (6 slices)

1½ cups shredded sharp Cheddar cheese

1½ cups shredded Swiss cheese

2 to 3 tablespoons flour

2 to 3 tablespoons diced pimento, drained

3 to 4 sprigs fresh parsley, leaves only, chopped

8 eggs, beaten

1 cup milk

Heat oven to 350° F.

Prepare bacon—bottled bacon pieces (sold by Hormel) can be used. Butter a 1½-quart casserole. Place cheeses in a medium bowl and add flour; toss using two spoons or clean hands until cheese shreds are coated with flour. Place cheese in casserole. Sprinkle bacon over cheese. Dot bacon and cheese with pieces of pimento and parsley leaves. Beat eggs and milk together. Pour over ingredients in the casserole.

Bake 25 to 30 minutes, or until puffed and starting to brown. It will smell invitingly of cheese.

Cooks' Notes

Thanks to the flour coating the cheese, the puff does not fall. If a portion or two is left over, chill and reheat later in the microwave. You can also use the microwave to reheat the omelet if someone oversleeps. If your family enjoys breakfast food at supper time, remember this high-protein casserole; it's excellent with a mixed green salad.

Menu Idea!

A FESTIVE BREAKFAST FOR ANY WEEKEND OF THE YEAR

Pineapple-Orange Juice served in wine glasses

Cheese-Rich Oven Omelet

Favorite Muffins or Coffee Cake

Fruit Plate of Berries on a Fan of Melon Slices

Southwest Egg Puff

This dish is another favorite from my now-closed bed-and-breakfast. It is high in protein yet has no meat, making it acceptable for vegetarians. In keeping with the Tex-Mex theme, I suggest serving corn muffins or corn bread with honey. Colleague Heather Randall King included it in *Savor the Flavor of the Edina Country Club* (1996). This recipe makes a nice, light main dish for a luncheon or a supper. Serve with a platter of sliced tomatoes and cucumbers, a hot green vegetable such as asparagus spears or whole green beans, and biscuits. If your family is adamant about eating meat, you could add a cup or so of diced cooked chicken or turkey to the cheese mixture.

MAKES 6 SERVINGS

10 eggs
½ cup all-purpose flour
1 teaspoon baking powder
Dash of salt
½ cup butter or margarine, melted
4-ounce can mild green chilies, chopped
12-ounce carton cottage cheese (1 ½ cups)
1 pound Monterey Jack cheese, shredded (4 cups)
Sour cream and salsa for topping

Heat oven to 350° F.

Grease a large casserole (9-by-13-inches or 10-inch square). In a large bowl, beat eggs until lemon colored and fluffy. Fold in the flour, baking powder, salt, melted butter, chilies, and both cheeses. Pour the egg-cheese mixture into prepared casserole.

Bake 35 to 50 minutes or until set. Let stand about 10 minutes before serving. Make a pattern with dollops of sour cream and salsa atop the casserole for an attractive presentation. Pass bowls of sour cream and salsa at the table so that guests can help themselves.

 **Variation**

Small-Family Egg Puff: Use half of each ingredient and bake the puff in a 1½-quart baking dish.

Baked Oatmeal Wisconsin-Style

In the past, many a mother in the Midwest, mine included, served hot cereal every school day morning during cold weather. Oatmeal got the nod most days, with Cream of Wheat, Cocoa Wheats, and Hot Ralston making an occasional appearance. Mom let my brother Bob and me sprinkle our bowls of oatmeal with generous amounts of brown sugar. Other lucky kids melted a pat of butter in the center of the hot mixture. As an adult, I pour on a couple tablespoons of half-and-half to add a rich flavor. I first tasted this oven oatmeal in Lake Geneva, Wisconsin, at their conference center. Big pans of cinnamon-flavored cereal awaited my group of Elderhostelers one morning before a class on Winston Churchill. This is a family-size version of the recipe. It works well for a Saturday or Sunday breakfast when you have houseguests. It's especially welcome to those who limit eggs because they are watching their cholesterol.

MAKES 4 TO 6 SERVINGS

OATMEAL

1¾ cups water

⅛ teaspoon salt

1 cup old fashioned or quick oats

CASSEROLE

2 eggs

⅔ cup milk

1 teaspoon cinnamon

1 teaspoon baking powder

¼ teaspoon salt

½ cup brown sugar

Heat oven to 350° F.

Bring water and salt to boil in saucepan. Stir in oats and cook 5 minutes, until thick. Set aside while combining remaining ingredients. (If desired, oatmeal can be cooked the night before. Just cover and refrigerate, then reheat in microwave before making casserole.)

Beat together eggs and milk. Stir cinnamon, baking powder, salt, and brown sugar into warm oatmeal, then fold in egg mixture. Pour into buttered or oil-sprayed 1½-quart casserole.

Bake 30 to 40 minutes, until set and a cinnamon-sugar crust forms on top. Serve with milk or half-and-half.

 ## Variation

Fruited Baked Oatmeal: Stir ⅔ to ¾ cup dark or golden raisins, chopped dates, or craisins (dried sweetened cranberries) into oatmeal mixture before baking.

Potato Hot Dish

Some folks simply won't eat eggs. But they can make a morning meal on hash brown potatoes and bacon, sausage, or ham. This casserole is for them. It makes a nice addition to a brunch spread, too. Or take it to a suppertime potluck.

MAKES 6 SERVINGS

¾ cup minced onion

2 teaspoons butter

4 cups cooked potatoes, peeled and diced (two 15-ounce cans sliced or whole potatoes can be used)

8 slices bacon, cooked and diced

1 cup diced American process cheese, such as Velveeta (4 ounces)

¼ cup thin-sliced, pimento-stuffed green olives

½ cup mayonnaise

Heat oven to 350° F.

Cook onion in butter in a small bowl in the microwave or in a small skillet on the stove. Combine onion, potatoes, bacon, cheese, olives, and mayonnaise in mixing bowl, stirring until potatoes are well coated with mayonnaise. Turn mixture into an 8-inch square baking dish.

Bake 35 to 45 minutes, until bubbly.

 **Variations**

Reduced-Fat Potato Hot Dish: Replace half the mayonnnaise with low fat yogurt or no-fat sour cream.

Big Batch Potato Hot Dish: Double all ingredients. Bake in 9-by-13-inch pan.

Do-Ahead Potato Hot Dish: Mix ingredients the night before, then cover and refrigerate until morning; may need to bake a few minutes longer.

Warm, Wonderful Desserts

LIFE IS UNCERTAIN...EAT DESSERT FIRST! This was the title of a little book someone gave me in the 1990s. It was an essay on joyfulness. Though it did include a few dessert recipes, its message was take joy where you find it—a serving of dessert is a good place to start. The title turned conventional practice on its head. Dessert first? Wow! I don't have to finish that spinach to earn it?

First or last, mid-afternoon or mid-evening, dessert brings joy. And it's ever so easy when you bake that sweet treat alongside a hot dish. Or you can slide it into the oven after the casserole comes out, baking it while you're eating the main course. The recipes in this small collection are homey, old-time desserts, most of them featuring fruits. All of them bring joy when I serve them to family and friends.

Mom's Bread Pudding

My late mother was strongly influenced by the Great Depression, which cast a pall over the family clothing and food budgets during the 1930s, only to be replaced by rationing during World War II. She was a dutiful cook, finding inspiration only when she and my dad, an Iowa weekly newspaper publisher, entertained guests. Tight budget or no, dessert was the reward for cleaning one's plate, and this was a favorite. She often made it with her luscious home-canned Colorado peaches. I still remember canning time, those long, steamy afternoons in the kitchen "doing up" fruit and tomatoes.

MAKES 6 SERVINGS

1½ cups milk

2 tablespoons butter

6 cups bread cubes

2 cups canned peaches, cut in chunks, or 16-ounce can fruit cocktail, drained

½ cup raisins

2 eggs

½ cup sugar

½ teaspoon vanilla

½ teaspoon cinnamon or nutmeg

¼ teaspoon salt

Heat the milk to scalding in a 2-quart saucepan. Add butter to pan. Set off the heat to cool while measuring other ingredients—butter melts in milk.

Heat oven to 350° F.

Grease a 2-quart casserole. Place bread cubes, peach chunks, and raisins in large bowl. Pour warm milk mixture over bread mixture; stir until all bread is moistened. In a medium bowl, beat the eggs and add the sugar, vanilla, cinnamon or nutmeg, and salt. Beat until the sugar is dissolved in the egg mixture. Add to the bread-and-milk mixture; mix well. Spoon the mixture into the casserole, making sure fruit is distributed evenly.

Bake uncovered about 1 hour or until knife inserted in center comes out clean. Serve warm with cream (half–and–half in a pitcher).

Cooks' Notes

When there's a bowl of this in the refrigerator, I like to reheat a portion in the microwave oven to savor as part of breakfast.

Variation

Chocolate Bread Pudding: Use chocolate milk in place of regular white milk. Substitute ¾ cup chocolate chips, ½ cup chopped pecans, and ⅓ cup halved maraschino cherries for peaches and raisins.

Menu Idea!

THE KITCHEN SMELLS WONDERFUL

Salmon Supreme (recipe page 78)

Tossed Green Salad with Cherry Tomatoes

Mom's Bread Pudding

Caramel Fruit Pudding

Cooks are always fascinated by a dessert that involves one part (the batter) changing places with another part (the sauce) during baking. Some sort of magic is going on there. It happens with chocolate batter and sauce in Oh, Fudge Pudding (recipe page 158) and it happens here with a fruit-studded batter and a brown sugar sauce.

MAKES 9 SERVINGS

1¼ cups brown sugar, divided

2 cups apple cider

2 tablespoons butter, margarine, or vegetable oil

½ cup milk

1¼ cups buttermilk biscuit mix

1 cup drained canned peach, apricot, or pear chunks

⅔ cup chopped nuts (optional)

Heat oven to 350° F.

Combine ¾ cup of the brown sugar, cider, and butter or oil in small saucepan. Bring to a boil and cook, stirring, 5 minutes. Pour brown sugar syrup into 1½-quart round baking dish. In a medium bowl, make a batter by combining the remaining ½ cup brown sugar, milk, biscuit mix, peaches, and if using, nuts. Using two spoons, drop batter on top of brown sugar syrup.

Bake 45 minutes or until batter has settled to bottom and pudding/topping is done. Serve warm.

 Cooks' Notes

For a smaller version, use ½ cup biscuit mix with ½ of all other ingredients, following directions above. Bake in an 8- or 9-inch loaf pan.

Menu Idea!

EVERYONE-PITCHES-IN SUPPER

The cook prepares the pudding while others make sandwiches, put out accompaniments, and set the table.

Ham, Lettuce, and Tomato Sandwiches

Potato or Corn Chips and Crisp Vegetable Relishes

Caramel Peach Pudding

Clafouti

Wisconsin-born food writer Patricia Wells introduced me to the delights of cla-fouti. The idea comes from peasant cooks in France, where Wells now lives, researches, cooks, and writes. She and her husband Walter, editor of the Paris-based *International Herald Tribune,* live in the French capitol during the week and spend weekends at their second home in southern France. Simply spread the fruit in a round pie plate, pour the pancake-like batter over it, and bake. Thanks to the availability of imported fresh fruits from all over the world, we can serve this classy dessert any time of year.

MAKES 6 SERVINGS

1 pound fresh dark sweet cherries, pitted, or 2 cups drained canned cherries
½ cup plus 2 tablespoons all-purpose unbleached flour
Dash of salt
3 large eggs
2 cups milk
¼ cup plus 2 tablespoons sugar
Powdered sugar for garnish

Heat oven to 350° F.

Butter or oil-spray a 10-inch deep-dish pie pan—make sure it has a capacity of 6 cups. Scatter cherries in the pan. Measure the flour and salt into a bowl and break the eggs on top. Using a kitchen fork, beat just the eggs lightly, then slowly beat in the flour a little at a time, making a smooth batter. Gradually stir in the milk, then the sugar. Pour the egg mixture over the cherries.

Bake the clafouti until puffed and golden around the edges, 40 to 45 minutes. Clafouti will sink as it cools. Just before serving, sprinkle lightly with pow-dered sugar—put a little powdered sugar in a small sieve and shake over the dessert.

 Variations

Pear Clafouti: Use 2 large pears, peeled and diced, in place of cherries.

Plum Clafouti: Use 2 cups diced plums instead of cherries.

Fruit-ful Cobbler

The Rhubarb Cobbler below is my favorite of the versions. For many in the Midwest, rhubarb is a "free" food. You buy a house and find a patch of rhubarb in the back someplace. Spring comes, you cut it and cook it—rhubarb sauce is, for many, the traditional spring tonic. Long ago, I planted Canadian red rhubarb not far from my back door and enjoyed the stalks for years.

MAKES 8 SERVINGS

FRUIT FILLING VARIATIONS:

RHUBARB FILLING

¾ cup sugar

2 tablespoons cornstarch

1 cup orange juice

2 teaspoons fresh or dried, grated orange rind

4 cups 1-inch pieces fresh rhubarb

BLUEBERRY OR BLACKBERRY FILLING

½ cup sugar

1 tablespoon cornstarch

1 teaspoon lemon juice

¼ cup water

4 cups fresh or frozen blueberries or blackberries

PEACH FILLING

½ cup sugar

1 tablespoon cornstarch

⅛ cup water

¼ teaspoon cinnamon

Dash of nutmeg or ground ginger

4 cups sliced, peeled peaches or 16-ounce bag frozen dry pack peach slices, thawed

CHERRY FILLING

1¼ cups sugar

3 tablespoons cornstarch

¼ cup water

¼ teaspoon almond extract

4 cups pitted fresh or frozen dry pack tart red cherries, thawed

COBBLER

1 cup all-purpose unbleached flour

2 tablespoons sugar

1½ teaspoons baking powder

¼ teaspoon salt

¼ cup vegetable oil, such as canola

1 egg, slightly beaten

¼ cup milk

½ teaspoon vanilla

Heat oven to 400° F.

First, cook filling (see variations above). Combine sugar, cornstarch, liquid, and seasonings in medium saucepan. Add fruit. If using rhubarb, do not add fruit until after the 1 minute simmering period; simply stir in rhubarb and cover pan to keep warm. For the other fruits, cook and stir over medium heat until mixture comes to a boil and thickens. Simmer, stirring constantly, 1 minute. Pour into 8-inch square glass baking dish or 2-quart baking dish. Place fruit in oven.

For cobbler, stir together flour, sugar, baking powder, and salt in large bowl. In separate bowl, combine oil, egg, milk, and vanilla. Add egg mixture all at once to dry ingredients. Stir just until moistened. Remove baking dish from oven. Drop dough in 8 spoonfuls atop hot fruit.

Bake 15 to 20 minutes or until golden brown. Serve warm.

New-Fashioned Fruit Crisp

This is my dessert of choice during February, when we turn to cherry desserts as a way of celebrating the birthday of George Washington. Though historians now doubt that young George was involved in the oft-repeated cherry tree story, we will forever link him with that tree and its fruit.

MAKES 8 TO 10 SERVINGS

1 (21-ounce) can cherry pie filling

4 cups canned or fresh fruit, drained and diced large
(such as peaches, pears, pineapple tidbits, bananas, apples, oranges)*

¼ cup coarsely chopped walnuts or pecans

1½ cups low fat granola (no raisins)

2–3 tablespoons melted butter or margarine

Fat-free vanilla yogurt

*I keep a 15-ounce can of fruit cocktail and an 8-ounce can of mandarin oranges, along with the pie filling, in the cupboard for the days when I decide to fix this on short notice. Dried fruit can be used as part of 4-cup total, too: dates, raisins, dried cranberries. This is a good way to use up odds and ends of fruit in the refrigerator.

Heat oven to 350° F.

Pour pie filling into a 2½-quart casserole dish. Fold in fruit and nuts. Sprinkle with granola and drizzle with melted butter.

Bake 40 minutes or until bubbling and hot throughout. Serve warm topped with yogurt (half-and-half is good, too). Leftovers reheat well in microwave.

 Variations

Apple Crisp: Use apple pie filling in place of cherry. If apple slices are large, use your kitchen shears to cut slices into smaller pieces.

Blueberry Crisp: Substitute blueberry pie filling for cherry. This variation is not quite as eye appealing as the others because the blueberries tend to turn the other fruits purple/blue during cooking.

 Cooks' Notes

Though I prefer granola with raisins for snacking, it does not work with this dessert. The raisins puff up and then burn, which smells bad and looks worse.

Oh, Fudge Pudding

Years ago, I lived in a modest bungalow, so small the dining room was comfortable for four, crowded for six, and impossible for eight. Nonetheless, I invited friends from our church to come for supper. These friends had four young sons—delightful boys whose antics the parents shared in an endless stream of anecdotes. How to serve eight people? I made a hot dish and this dessert and stowed them in the oven. Made a salad, probably gelatin with fruit, and had that ready in the refrigerator. Cleaned up the kitchen and set the kitchen table for the boys and set the dining room table for us grown-ups. My cozy kitchen proved a great novelty for the boys, who lived in a sprawling suburban house. And the youngest, then barely 3, couldn't get enough of this pudding. "Pooding!" he said. "More pooding!" We ate up every lick.

MAKES 9 SERVINGS

1 cup all-purpose unbleached flour

2 teaspoons baking powder

¼ teaspoon salt

1¾ cups brown sugar, divided

¼ cup plus 2 tablespoons baking cocoa, divided

½ cup milk

2 tablespoons vegetable oil

½ to 1 cup chopped nuts

1¾ cups hot strong coffee

Heat oven to 350° F.

Stir flour, baking powder, salt, ¾ cup of the brown sugar, and 2 tablespoons of the cocoa together in a medium bowl. Add milk and oil and stir well. Fold in nuts. Pour into 9-inch square baking dish or pan. Combine remaining 1 cup brown sugar and ¼ cup baking cocoa; sprinkle cocoa mixture over batter in pan. Pour hot coffee over batter.

Bake 45 minutes, until pudding pulls away from sides of pan. While it bakes, pudding rises to top and chocolate sauce goes to the bottom. Serve warm.

Cooks' Notes

If you do not have a 9-inch square pan, use an 8-inch square, but keep an eye on it as it will be very full. Baking may take a few minutes longer since batter is deeper.

A LESSON ON LEAVENING

Handle baking powder (used in puddings like this, cobblers, and biscuit-topped casseroles) with care. Once it comes in contact with liquid, it starts to work. It's fine to measure out and mix ingredients for these toppings ahead of time, but the minute the dry ingredients are mixed with wet (be it water or milk), it has to go right in the oven. And never substitute baking powder for soda. There are two reasons: first, 1 teaspoon baking powder contains only about ¼ teaspoon soda, so it's not a real substitution; second, acid ingredients, such as buttermilk, require soda (bicarbonate of soda) to balance that acid.

Pear on the Square

I'm guessing that many an American kitchen cupboard contains a can of pears, peaches, apricots, or fruit cocktail. Ready and waiting for a simple recipe like this one. When you find a few minutes to stir up a little extra something, here's a treat to slip into the oven alongside a favorite hot dish. It makes eight servings but if your household is smaller, that's not a problem. This sweet keeps nicely. Try a square of it mid-afternoon with a cup of restoring tea. It will ease whatever strain the day has brought. Or, better yet, phone a neighbor and share the treat and the tea.

MAKES 8 SQUARE SERVINGS

15-ounce can pears

2 eggs

1 cup granulated sugar

2 teaspoons vanilla

¾ cup chopped nuts, preferably walnuts

½ cup all-purpose unbleached flour

2 teaspoons baking powder

½ teaspoon salt

Heat oven to 350° F.

Drain pears; cut them into 1-inch chunks. Heavily grease or line with kitchen parchment paper a 7-by-11-inch baking pan. Beat eggs well. Add sugar and beat until smooth. Stir in vanilla, pears, and nuts. Stir flour, baking powder, and salt together (I do this on waxed paper to save a bowl). Fold flour mixture into fruit batter. Pour into prepared pan.

Bake 25 to 35 minutes until golden and sweet-smelling.

 **Variations**

Peach on the Square: Use well-drained sliced canned peaches.

Apricots on the Square: Use drained diced apricots.

Fruit Cocktail Squares: Use well-drained fruit cocktail.

Menu Idea!

SUPPER TO BRIGHTEN A GRAY DAY

Your Choice of *Hot Dish Heaven's*
Ground Beef Casseroles

Cole Slaw with Diced Cucumber and Peanuts

Scandinavian Whole Grain Crisp-Bread

Pear on the Square

Phoebe's Peach Noodle Kugel

Years ago I volunteered with Minneapolis's Theatre in the Round Players, helping with costumes and props for this popular community theater. After all the pressure of the rehearsals, including getting the set built and the costumes fitted, and the excitement of the performances, came the fun of the cast party. This time the late Phoebe and Joe Franken, both talented performers, hosted the party at their St. Louis Park home. And Phoebe prepared her cinnamon-topped kugel. It was the first time I had tasted this traditional Jewish dessert and I loved it immediately. Though busy as a real estate saleswoman and mother of two boys, Phoebe wrote up the directions for me. At the time, her younger son, Alan, though still in grade school, was performing on stage and in commercials, experience that led to his present-day career as a writer and radio personality. Now he's just Al Franken.

MAKES 12 TO 15 SERVINGS

8 ounces uncooked medium egg noodles (about 3 cups dry noodles)

4 eggs, well beaten

½ cup granulated sugar

½ teaspoon salt

2 cups creamed cottage cheese

2 cups sour cream

¼ cup butter, melted

about 4 cups drained, canned peach slices (two 15-ounce cans)

Cinnamon

Granulated sugar

Heat oven to 350° F.

Cook noodles as directed on package. Drain noodles; place in buttered 13-by-9-inch pan. Fold together beaten eggs, sugar, salt, cottage cheese, sour cream, and melted butter. Pour egg mixture over noodles. Arrange drained peach slices, placing them closely in rows, atop ingredients in pan. Sprinkle lightly with cinnamon and sugar.

Bake uncovered 45 to 50 minutes or until knife inserted in center comes out clean.

Baked Rice Custard

When I hear the words nursery food, rice custard is one of two foods I think of. Soft foods, easy to digest yet nutritious, are ideal both for little children and for aging elders. (The other nursery special is milk toast: hot milk poured over a piece of buttered, cinnamon-sugared toast.)

I'm also reminded of a favorite A. A. Milne poem, "Rice Pudding," from *When We Were Very Young* (New York: Dutton, [1924] 1988). Here's how it goes: "What is the matter with Mary Jane? She's crying with all her might and main, And she won't eat her dinner—rice pudding, again—What is the matter with Mary Jane?" By the fifth verse, it's clear that she is oh-so-tired of rice pudding. The drawing, by the inimitable Ernest H. Shepard, shows a little girl with a big hair bow in a high chair willfully kicking off her shoe—a Mary Jane, of course.

MAKES 8 SERVINGS

2 cups cooked white rice

4 eggs, beaten

¼ cup honey or ⅓ cup granulated or brown sugar

2 cups milk

¾ cup half-and-half or evaporated milk

¼ teaspoon salt

1 teaspoon grated orange peel

2 teaspoons vanilla

Grated nutmeg for garnish

Heat oven to 350° F.

Using a medium bowl, mix rice, eggs, honey or sugar, milk, half-and-half, salt, orange peel, and vanilla. Turn into a buttered 1½-quart baking dish. Set dish into a pan filled with hot water to within 1 inch of the top. Handle the pan and dish carefully as you put it in the oven to prevent spilling the hot water.

Bake custard 50 to 60 minutes, stirring once half way through the baking time. Remove from water bath. Sprinkle top with grated nutmeg. After serving, refrigerate any leftovers.

 ## Variations

Rice Custard with Raisins: Stir ⅓ cup dark or golden raisins or craisins (dried cranberries) into custard mixture.

Swedish Rice Custard: Sprinkle top of custard with slivered almonds during last 10 minutes of baking; omit nutmeg.

Menu Idea!

SUPPER TO PLEASE THE NURSERY SET

Oven-Fried Chicken Legs

Mashed Potatoes

Pear Face Salad with Shredded Cheese Hair
(canned pear half is the face with raisin features
and cheese shreds around top as hair)

Hot Biscuits with Marmalade

Baked Rice Custard

Appendix

Cream Sauce

Many sources call this White Sauce, due to the white color of the milk. But I'm using Cream Sauce despite the fact that it is made with milk, not cream, because it looks creamy when finished. Soup manufacturers call their products "cream of whatever" soup though they're made with milk, presumably because their formulas were based on old-time creamed soup recipes that were indeed made with cream. If you're so inclined, use one cup of the Thick Cream Sauce below in place of a can of condensed cream soup in favorite hot dish recipes.

MAKES 1 CUP

THIN SAUCE

1 tablespoon butter, margarine, or oil

1½ tablespoons flour

¼ teaspoon salt

Dash of teaspoon black or white pepper or paprika

1 cup milk

MEDIUM SAUCE

2 tablespoons butter, margarine, or oil

3 tablespoons flour

½ teaspoon salt

⅛ teaspoon black or white pepper or paprika

1 cup milk

THICK SAUCE

3 tablespoons butter, margarine, or oil

4 tablespoons flour

½ teaspoon salt

⅛ teaspoon black or white pepper or paprika

1 cup milk

Melt the butter in saucepan over medium heat. Stir in the flour, salt, and pepper. Cook 1 to 2 minutes, stirring constantly—a wire whisk is best—until smooth and bubbly. (Flour mixture must be cooked 1 additional minute at this point to avoid a floury taste in the finished sauce.) Remove pan from heat. Pour in milk. Stir constantly, cook until smooth and boiling. Use as directed.

 **Variations**

Cheese Sauce: Remove Cream Sauce from heat and stir in 1 cup shredded natural sharp Cheddar cheese.

Cream Sauce for Poultry Hot Dishes: Use half chicken broth and half milk in sauce.

Pastry Crust

1½ cups all-purpose unbleached flour

½ teaspoon salt

¼ cup plus 2 tablespoons soft shortening, such as Crisco

3 to 4 tablespoons ice cold water

MAKES 1 LARGE CRUST

Sift flour before measuring. Measure flour and salt into mixing bowl; stir together with fork. Drop shortening by tablespoonfuls onto flour. Taking a pastry blender in one hand and holding the bowl firmly in the other, cut the shortening into the flour until mixture looks like coarse meal. Place about ⅓ cup ice water in a cup. Using a one tablespoon measure, add 1 tablespoon of ice water to flour in bowl, then mix it in with fork. Repeat this twice.

If all flour has not been moistened, add 1 more tablespoon water, working dough until it forms a ball. Using clean hands, round up ball of pastry dough. Arrange a pastry cloth on a work surface (I use my dining room table) and dust lightly with flour. Have ready a rolling pin covered with stockinette and also dusted with flour. Place dough ball in center of cloth and roll dough into a circle, working back and forth to produce a round that is uniform in thickness.

Hold pan for pie over pastry circle to be sure it is large enough to cover pan with at least one inch extra for finishing edge. Fold pastry into quarters. Carefully lift pastry into place atop filled pie pan. Unfold pastry adjusting placement on pan. Fold pastry edge under, forming a thick edge around rim of pan.

Using your thumb and forefinger, pinch pastry edge every 2 inches or so to give a pie a crimped edging. To protect pastry rim from over-browning, tear three narrow strips of aluminum foil and shape them around pastry edging. This covering must be removed after 25 to 30 minutes of baking so edge turns golden.

Remember, if time is short, use pre-rolled refrigerated pie crust.

Index

Permissions

In "Casserole Classics," the recipe for Beef Stew the Oven Way (aka Football Stew) is from *Foxy Ladies* by Ellen Kort, copyright © 1981 by Ellen Kort. Used by permission of Ellen Kort, Appleton WI.

In "Round the World in a Casserole Dish," the recipe for Diana's Moctezuma Pie is from *The Essential Cuisines of Mexico* by Diana Kennedy, copyright © 2000 by Diana Kennedy. Used by permission of Clarkson Potter/Publishers, a division of Random House Inc.

The recipe for Tian of Zucchini, Rice, and Cheese is from *The World of Cheese* by Evan Jones, copyright © 1976 by Evan Jones and Judith B. Jones. Used by permission of Judith B. Jones.

In "Hot Dishes for Potlucks and Church Suppers," the recipe for Enchilada Fiesta is from *Recipes from South Dakota . . . with love* by Laurie Gluesing and Debra Gluesing, copyright © 1986 by Gluesing and Gluesing. Used by permission of Gluesing and Gluesing.

The design & typsetting of *Hot Dish Heaven* was cooked up by Percolator Graphic Design in Minneapolis. Among the ingredients are the typefaces Tiki, Paperback, and Futura. Final presentation was done by Maple Press, York, Pennsylvania.